EARLY GENERATIONS

OF THE

Founders of Old Dunstable

THIRTY FAMILIES

EZRA S. STEARNS, A. M.

AUTHOR OF

HISTORY OF RINDGE, N. H.; HISTORY OF ASHBURNHAM, MASS.;
HISTORY OF PLYMOUTH, N. H.

CLEARFIELD

Originally published
Boston, Massachusetts, 1911

Reprinted for
Clearfield Company, Inc. by
Genealogical Publishing Co., Inc.
Baltimore, Maryland
2000

International Standard Book Number: 0-8063-5039-3

CONTENTS.

ACRES FAMILY,	1
BEALE FAMILY,	1
BLANCHARD FAMILY,	3
COOKE FAMILY,	14
CROMWELL FAMILY,	16
DARBEYSHIRE FAMILY,	17
FRENCH FAMILY,	18
GALUSHA FAMILY,	21
GOULD FAMILY,	25
HARWOOD FAMILY,	27
HASSELL FAMILY,	29
HONEY FAMILY,	31
LOVEWELL FAMILY,	33
LUND FAMILY,	47
MARKS FAMILY,	55
PARRIS FAMILY,	56
PERRY FAMILY,	59
READ FAMILY,	60
ROBBINS FAMILY,	62
SEARLES FAMILY,	64
SMITH FAMILY,	65
SWALLOW FAMILY,	67
TAYLOR FAMILY,	74
TEMPLE FAMILY,	81
TYNG FAMILY,	82
USHER FAMILY,	88
WALDO FAMILY,	90
WARNER FAMILY,	91
WELD FAMILY,	91
WHITING FAMILY,	93

PREFACE.

DUNSTABLE was granted by Massachusetts and was a part of that province until 1741, when a revision of the province line transferred the greater part of the original grant to the jurisdiction of New Hampshire. The early families of this ancient town at the time it was cut in twain were living in Nashua, and parts of Hollis, Hudson, Litchfield and Merrimack in New Hampshire and in Dunstable and Tyngsborough in Massachusetts. The early records of legislation, civil and military appointments, land titles and probate court are preserved in the archives of Massachusetts. The condition of jurisdiction and the division of the original grant into several townships will find frequent application in the following pages.

I have read Fox's History of Dunstable many times and with unfailing interest. It is a vivid portraiture of an ancient and prominent town. It was written sixty-five years ago and at a time when little attention was given to genealogy. A regret that Fox did not extend the family records is attended with gratitude that he saved so much from the accumulating chronicles of oblivion.

At the beginning of King William's War, on account of a well founded fear of the Indians, a majority of the families of the settlement, about 1695, fled from Dunstable to the older and better fortified towns. In some instances it was a temporary absence, but John Acres, Samuel Beale, Benjamin Beale, Andrew Cooke, John Lovewell, senior, Joseph Lovewell, Patrick Marks and Christopher Read subsequently sold their farms and did not return to Dunstable. This fact accounts for the brevity of the record of several families.

Genealogies of the Adams, Cummings, Danforth, Fletcher, Hunt, Richardson and Whitney families are published and are easily accessible to all. For this reason these families are not included in this volume. The New England Historic Genealogical Register contains sketches of four Dunstable families; reference is made to "The Butterfields of Middlesex," by George A. Gordon, A. M., Register, 1890; "Captain Edward Johnson of Woburn, Mass., and his descendants," by Hon. Edward Francis Johnson, Register, 1905; "John Solendine of Dunstable" by Ethel Stanwood Bolton, B. A., Register, 1906; "The Woods Family of Groton, Mass.," by Henry Ernest Woods, A. M., Register, 1910.

In the preparation of this volume a constant effort has been made to collect and transcribe the date of births and deaths and the record of marriages, but the sketches of individuals are purposely very brief. A fitting biography of several of the persons named in these pages would fill a volume.

To Otis G. Hammond of the State Library, Edward N. Pearson, Secretary of State, Dr. Irving A. Watson, Register of Vital Statistics, all of Concord, I plead guilty to a chronic obligation. Their willing and frequent assistance has renewed and strengthened the friendship of many years.

For the register of the Blanchard family, Mrs. Louisa Bethune of Buffalo, New York, and for the record of the descendants of Joseph Lovewell, Prof. Samuel Harrison Lovewell of Quincy, Illinois, have made valuable contributions which will be appreciated and esteemed by the readers of this volume.

Joined with these, whom I recall with gratitude, are George S. Stewart, an accomplished genealogist, Rodney P. Wright of Cambridge, Mass., and Rev. Thomas M. Corson of Salem, Mass., who have cheerfully responded to many inquiries. With a voice of thankfulness these lines are spoken.

EZRA S. STEARNS.

Fitchburg, Mass., 1911.

THIRTY DUNSTABLE FAMILIES.

1. JOHN ACRES in 1664 was living at Muddy River, an ancient name of Brookline, and then a part of Boston. A way passing through the land of John Acres was confirmed July 31, 1671. Against his name on the tax list of Muddy River in 1674, is written "Gone," but his name appears in a list of residents dated in August of the same year. He married Desire Y* Truth Thorne, baptized in Roxbury, March 23, 1644, a daughter of William and Mary Thorne of Muddy River. She was admitted to the church in Roxbury, July 8, 1666. The family removed to Dunstable before 1680. A few months after a church was gathered "Sister Accor" was dismissed from the church in Roxbury to the church in Dunstable, April 4, 1686. In 1682, John Acres was chosen "to pound, youke and Ring the hogs of Dunstable three months ould and upward." He lived in Dunstable about fifteen years and acquired a considerable quantity of land. He returned to Boston about 1695. The name in early records is written Acres, Acrees, Accor, Acker and Akers.

Six children were baptized at Roxbury, the birth of three of these is on record at Boston and the two youngest were born at Dunstable.

   i   ELIZABETH, born May 18, 1664; baptized July 15, 1666; died July 24, 1666.
   ii. DESIRE Y* TRUTH, born March 9, 1665-6; baptized July 15, 1666.
   iii. ELIZABETH, born November 24, 1668; baptized November 29, 1668.
   iv. DEBORAH, baptized, February 26, 1670-1.
   v. JOHN, baptized August 10, 1673.
   vi. WILLIAM, baptized May 29, 1679.
   vii. MARY, born May 26, 1682.
   viii. JOANNA, born January 10, 1684-5.

1. WILLIAM BEALE, born about 1628, was a prominent citizen of Marblehead, Mass. He died 1694. His will

dated January 4, 1693-4, was proved May 21, 1694. He was a miller and he bought and sold many parcels of land. At an early date he owned a tract of land in Dunstable, which was occupied and improved by two of his sons.

He married Martha Bradstreet, born 1632, daughter of Humphrey and Bridget Bradstreet of Ipswich. She died April 6, 1675; he married, second, December 16, 1676, Elizabeth Jackson, widow of Edmund Jackson. She died November 5, 1683, he married, third, March 4, 1683-4, Mary Hart, widow of Samuel Hart. Fourteen children, of whom Samuel and William were residents of Dunstable.

2. SAMUEL BEALE, son of William and Martha (Bradstreet) Beale, was born in Marblehead, July 15, 1654. He married in Lynn, March 28, 1682, Patience Lovewell, daughter of John and Elizabeth (Sylvester) Lovewell, see. At the time of marriage he removed to Dunstable and while he remained he was a prominent factor of the settlement. He was town clerk, selectman and prominent in the affairs of the proprietors. It is evident that he was educated beyond the measure of his time. His ornate handwriting and accurate diction are conspicuous features of the early records of Dunstable. In 1693, and during King William's War he returned to Marblehead where he died 1699. Patience, his widow, married second, August 19, 1708, Archibald Ferguson. He was a scrivener. They were living in Marblehead in 1722. A record of their death is not found. Four children of Samuel and Patience Beale.

    i. ELIZABETH, baptized in Marblehead, April 19, 1685; married at Marblehead, December 23, 1703, John Grant, born August 31, 1682, son of Francis and Susannah (Combs) Grant of Marblehead.

    ii. SAMUEL, born at Dunstable, July 3, 1685, died young.

    iii. EBENEZER, born at Dunstable, January 30, 1687-8. Sidney Perley, in Essex Antiquarian, says he was a mariner living at Marblehead in 1709, and in 1723 was in London, England.

    iv. PATIENCE, baptized at Marblehead, February 21, 1696-7. She married Joseph Selman, a native of England. They lived in Marblehead. Their children were Archibald, Joseph, Samuel, Lovewell, Beale, William, John, Patience, and Mary.

Thirty Dunstable Families. 3

3. WILLIAM BEALE, son of William and Martha (Bradstreet) Beale was born in Marblehead, August 24, 1659. He married Elizabeth Lovewell, daughter of John and Elizabeth (Sylvester) Lovewell, see. He came to Dunstable 1684, and lived here about ten years, returning to Marblehead at the beginning of King William's War, when the settlement was nearly deserted. He died 1711. His will dated May 9, 1711, was proved June 27, 1711. Twelve children of William and Elizabeth Beale.

   i. ELIZABETH, baptized, Marblehead, September 7, 1684; died young.
   ii. WILLIAM, born, Dunstable, March 12, 1684-5; baptized May 24, 1696.
   iii. ELIZABETH, born, Dunstable, November 16, 1686; baptized May 24, 1696.
   iv. ZACCHEUS, baptized May 24, 1696.
   v. JOHN, baptized, May 24, 1696.
   vi. JAMES, baptized, May 24, 1696.
   vii. BRIDGET, baptized, May 24, 1696. One Bridget Beale married Peter Honey of Dunstable, see.
   viii. MARTHA, baptized May 24, 1696. One Martha Beale married Andrew Cooke, see.
   ix. ANNA, baptized, March 28, 1697.
   x. JOSEPH, baptized September 11, 1698.
   xi. PATIENCE, baptized November 16, 1701.
   xii. SARAH, baptized March 14, 1702-3.

1. DEA. JOHN BLANCHARD. It has been stated in print many times that Dea. John Blanchard of Dunstable was a son of Thomas Blanchard, the American ancestor of a numerous family. A son John is not named in the will of Thomas, and evidence recently discovered establishes the fact that Dea. John was a son of Widow Ann Blanchard, who died in Chelmsford, June 24, 1662. William Blanchard, the tailor, who died in Boston, October 7, 1652, probably was a brother of Dea. John. Dea. John Blanchard married about 1657, Elizabeth Hills, born 1627, a daughter of Joseph and Rose (Clark) Hills. For good service to the colony, 500 acres in Dunstable were granted to Joseph Hills, which in his will is bequeathed to his granddaughters, Hannah and Elizabeth Blanchard of Dunstable. Elizabeth (Hills) Blanchard died about 1662, and Dea. John Blanchard

married, second, Mrs. Hannah (Brackett) Kinsley, born in Braintree, 1634, a daughter of Dea. Richard and Alice Brackett and widow of Samuel Kinsley. Elizabeth Kinsley, child of Samuel and Hannah (Brackett) Kinsley, was the wife of John Cummings of Dunstable.

Dea. John Blanchard was one of the foundation members and the first deacon of the church of Dunstable and one of the most active and useful citizens. In the lives of his sons and his grandsons, his example was cherished and his good works were renewed. He died 1694. For his will see Granite Monthly, July, 1906. His widow Hannah, her daughter Elizabeth (Kinsley) Cummings, her son Nathaniel Blanchard with his wife, Lydia Blanchard, and Susannah, a daughter of Nathaniel and Lydia Blanchard, were slain at Dunstable by the Indians, July 3, 1706. There were two children of Dea. John and Elizabeth and nine of Dea. John and Hannah Blanchard.

    i.   HANNAH, born Charlestown, January 6, 1658-9; married 1679, Thomas Read of Chelmsford, see.

    ii. ELIZABETH, married Robert Parris; married second, 1710, Thomas Burrage of Lynn, Massachusetts. See Parris family.

    iii. JOSIAH, born March 15, 1665; died young.

    iv. BENJAMIN, born March 15, 1665, twin. He was living 1693.

2.   v.   JAMES, born March 10, 1666.

3.   vi. THOMAS, born 1668.

    vii. SARAH, born 1670; married January 23, 1694, Robert Usher, see.

4. viii. JOSEPH, born November 1, 1672.

    ix. MARY, born September 23, 1674; married John Derbyshire; married second, Nathaniel Woods. See Derbyshire family.

    x.   NATHANIEL, twin, born September 23, 1674. He and his wife, Lydia, and daughter, Susanna, were killed by the Indians July 3, 1706. His son, Nathaniel, born September 12, 1705, died young.

    xi. MARTHA, born 1676; died November 16, 1676.

2. JAMES BLANCHARD, son of Dea. John, was born March 10, 1666. He married Anna Blood, born March 1, 1671, daughter of Nathaniel and Hannah (Parker) Blood. He lived in Groton, Massachusetts, and was a town clerk several years. In December, 1703, and January, 1704, he was a soldier in the first snowshoe company, commanded by Capt. William Tyng. He died from fatigue

Thirty Dunstable Families. 5

and exposure in that service in February, 1704. See Granite State Magazine, April and May, 1906. Four children.

i. ELIZABETH, born June 29, 1694; married July 25, 1717, Benjamin Hazen, born, Rowley, February 19, 1694-5, son of Edward and Jane (Pickard) Hazen. He married second, April 2, 1740, Elizabeth Nutting. He died September 18, 1755. Three of the four children of Benjamin and Elizabeth (Blanchard) Hazen, died young. Their daughter Hepsibah, was born February 19, 1724-5.

ii. JOSIAH, born June 24, 1698. Lived in Concord, Massachusetts. He enlisted May 10, 1740, for the expedition to Carthagena in which very few survived. He married July 16, 1719, Mary Dudley, born at Concord, February 8, 1700, daughter of Joseph and Abigail (Goble) Dudley. Lived in Concord, where six children were born.

iii. ANNA, born March 11, 1701, married August 11, 1719, Moses Bennett. Lived in Groton. Eight children.

iv. EUNICE, born February 8, 1702-3; died April 3, 1710.

3. THOMAS BLANCHARD, son of Dea. John, born 1668. He lived in Woburn a few years and after 1693, again in Dunstable, where he died March 9, 1727. He married in Woburn, February 13, 1688-9, Tabitha Lepingwell, born in Woburn, May 8, 1661, daughter of Michael and Isabel Lepingwell. She died in Dunstable, November 29, 1696. He married, second, October 4, 1698, Ruth Adams, born at Chelmsford, March 8, 1673, daughter of Pelatiah and Ruth Adams. Five children by first, and eight by second wife.

i. TABITHA, born, Woburn, February 27, 1689; married September 30, 1719, Thomas Blodgett, son of Thomas and Mary (Parkhurst) Blodgett. They lived in Chelmsford and in Westford. He died 1730. She died March 1, 1764. Three children.

ii. HANNAH, born, Woburn, November 29, 1690.

iii. MARY, born, Woburn, September 6, 1692.

iv. ABIGAIL, born, Dunstable, May 5, 1694; married 1723, John Blodgett, born Chelmsford, November 26, 1698, son of Thomas and Mary (Druse) Blodgett. They lived at Chelmsford and Westford. Three children.

v. JOHN, born, Dunstable, May 20, 1696. He married at Groton, May 30, 1722, Mary Sawtell, born April 11, 1697, daughter of Zachariah and Mary (Blood) Sawtell. They lived in Chelmsford.

vi. THOMAS, born, Dunstable, August 12, 1699. He was captured by the Indians 1724. By wife Elizabeth, he had a son, Thomas, born October 20, 1724. A daughter, Hannah, married James Brown.

6   *Thirty Dunstable Families.*

   vii. WILLIAM, born 1701; died in infancy.
   viii. RUTH, born April 1, 1703.
   ix. ELIZABETH, born January 13, 1705.
   x. BENJAMIN, born December 28, 1706.
   xi. NATHANIEL, born September 30, 1709.
   xii. JAMES, born December 29, 1711.
   xiii. WILLIAM, born 1713; married at Groton, February 28, 1733-4, Deliverance Parker, born July 28, 1714, daughter of Nathaniel and Lydia Parker of Groton. The birth of two children recorded in Dunstable: (1) Olive, born November 4, 1734; (2) Nathaniel, born December 25, 1735.

4. CAPT. JOSEPH BLANCHARD, son of Dea. John, born November 1, 1672. He was a man of character and ability, and prominent in the affairs of Dunstable. He married May 25, 1696, Abiah Hassell, born May 13, 1673, daughter of Joseph and Anna (Perry) Hassell. He died in 1727. His widow died December 8, 1746. They were the parents of nine children.

   i. ELIZABETH, born April 15, 1697; married Dea. Jonathan Cummings, born July 3, 1703, son of Dea. Thomas and Priscilla (Warner) Cummings of Dunstable. They lived in Merrimack, where he died 1791. She died May 28, 1774. For a record of their six children, see Cummings Genealogy. Dea. Jonathan, not Josiah Cummings, as stated in the genealogy, was the soldier in Capt. Lovewell's third expedition who assisted his cousin, William Cummings, to his home.
   ii. ESTHER, born July 29, 1699; married Henry Farwell, son of Henry and Susannah (Richardson) Farwell. They lived in Dunstable. See Hill's Old Dunstable for record of the family.
   iii. HANNAH, born October 1, 1701; married John Usher, see.
5. iv. JOSEPH, born February 11, 1704.
   v. RACHEL, born March 23, 1705; died young.
   vi. SUSANNAH, born March 29, 1707; married Jonathan Farwell, born July 24, 1700, son of Henry and Susannah (Richardson) Farwell. See Hill's Old Dunstable.
   vii. JANE, born March 19, 1709; married Rev. Josiah Swan, born Charlestown, March 18, 1711-12, son of Ebenezer and Prudence (Foster) Swan. Ebenezer, the father, died in 1716, and Prudence, the mother, was the second wife of Rev. John Prentice of Lancaster. The son, Josiah, graduated at Harvard University, 1733, and was a school teacher at Lancaster, and was admitted to the church there, May 11, 1735. He was ordained and installed over the church at Dunstable, December 27, 1738. After his dismissal, 1746, he returned to Lancaster. He died in Wal-

Thirty Dunstable Families. 7

pole, Massachusetts. Record is found of two children: (1) John, died at Lancaster, June 7, 1751; (2) Frances, baptized at Lancaster, October 14, 1750.

viii. RACHEL, born March 21, 1712; married at Woburn, July 31, 1729, Joshua Converse, born in Woburn, June 3, 1704, son of John and Abigail (Sawyer) Converse. He was a soldier in Capt. Eleazer Tyng's company, 1725. They lived in Dunstable and later in Merrimack, where he was a moderator, assessor and selectman. He was drowned in the Merrimack river in 1744. She married, second, February 9, 1754, Joseph Fitch, born October 22, 1702, son of Samuel and Elizabeth (Walker) Fitch of Bedford, Massachusetts. He died February 7, 1769. She married third, June 3, 1773, John Paige, born October 11, 1704, son of Nathaniel and Susannah (Lane) Paige of Bedford. She died in Bedford, June 16, 1801. Her children were:

1. *Rachel Converse,* born in Leicester, Mass., April 30, 1730; married Timothy Taylor. See Taylor register.
2. *Joseph Converse,* born November 13, 1739; married May 27, 1762, Elizabeth Davis. He lived many years in Bedford. He was a soldier in the Revolution. In 1794, he removed to Chesterfield, N. H., where he died February 10, 1828. His wife died August 10, 1817. Among his descendants is Larkin G. Mead, the sculptor. See Converse Genealogy, by Rev. John Jay Putnam.
3. *Jesse Converse,* born December 31, 1741. He was a soldier in the French and Indian War. He was a Capt. Nehemiah Lovewell's company of Col. John Hart's regiment, 1758. He probably died in early manhood.
4. *Zebulon Converse,* born March 21, 1744. He settled in Rindge, N. H., and is the ancestor of a numerous and prominent family. See History of Rindge.
5. *Thaddeus Fitch,* born in Bedford, Mass., March 23, 1755. He lived a short time in Rindge and in Amherst, N. H. He was a quartermaster in Gen. Stark's Brigade, 1777. In 1778, he returned to Bedford. He married, September 14, 1779, Mary Moor. He died 1819. Three children.

ix. ELEAZER, born December 1, 1715; died April 29, 1717, per town records, but gravestone record of his death is April 20, 1718.

5. COL. JOSEPH BLANCHARD, son of Capt. Joseph, was born at Dunstable, February 11, 1704. He married at Groton, September 26, 1728, Rebecca Hubbard, born at Concord, February 11, 1710-11, daughter of Major Jonathan and Rebecca (Brown) Hubbard. She was a sister of the wife of Col. Josiah Willard, with whom Col. Blanchard was intimately associated. He was an educated man of superior intelligence and capacity. He served the town of Dunstable with ability and credit. He was commissioned a Colonel of the regiment of militia, which included a large area near his home,

from 1744 until his death, and maintaining intimate relations with Governor Benning Wentworth, he was entrusted with the assignment of troops from his regiment to exposed points at the north and west of Dunstable. In 1755, he commanded a regiment in the expedition to Crown Point. One of the companies of this regiment was commanded by Capt. Robert Rogers, with John Stark, lieutenant, who were renowned in the ranger service. In the provincial government he was appointed a mandamus councillor, but there is no record that he acted as such. In 1749, he was appointed a justice of the Superior Court and held the commission until his death.

He was the trusted agent of the Masonian Proprietors, and as attorney he made grants of several towns and from 1748 until his death his activities moulded the early history of many communities. He died April 7, 1758. His wife, Rebecca, died April 17, 1774. Gravestones in the old burying ground at Dunstable. They had thirteen children born at Dunstable.

6.   i. JOSEPH, born April 28, 1729.
    ii. ELEAZER, born November 15, 1730; died March 19, 1753.
    iii. SUSANNAH, twin, born November 15, 1730; died before 1758.
    iv. REBECCA, born July 20, 1732; married James Minot.
    v. SARAH, born October 7, 1734; died young.
    vi. CATHERINE, born November 15, 1736; married Rev. Elias Smith, born, Reading, Massachusetts, 1731, son of Benjamin and Elizabeth (Burnap) Smith. Harvard University, 1753. Pastor of church in Middleton, Massachusetts. He preached in Dunstable in 1757 and received a call but was not settled here. He died in Middleton, October 17, 1791. His wife died November 17, 1817. Nine children.

7. vii. JONATHAN, born September 18, 1738.
    viii. SARAH, born August 2, 1740; married September 17, 1761, Robert Fletcher, born 1727, son of Robert Fletcher of Tyngsboro. He lived in Dunstable. He was clerk of the court of Hillsborough county. He died September 9, 1793. His widow died March 29, 1798. Several children.
    ix. JAMES, born September 20, 1742.

8. x. JOTHAM, born 1744.
9. xi. AUGUSTUS, born July 29, 1746.
    xii. CALEB, born August 15, 1749; died young. The headstone is illegible.

Thirty Dunstable Families.

xiii. HANNAH, born October 21, 1751; married April 4, 1776, Dr. Ebenezer Starr, born, Dedham, May 1, 1744, son of Jonathan and Sarah (Dean) Starr. He was a physician of Dunstable, Massachusetts. His wife, Hannah, died March 22, 1794. He married second, Rebecca Blanchard, daughter of Hon. Jonathan Blanchard, see. Dr. Starr died September 7, 1798. His widow, Rebecca, died October 19, 1810. Six children of first and one of second wife. Rebecca, born June 8, 1777; died November 1, 1778; James Blanchard, born November 27, 1778; Ebenezer, born February 18, 1780; Hannah, born January 26, 1782; John, born December 30, 1783; Edward, born July 29, 1786; Augustus posthumous, born March 3, 1799.

6. JOSEPH BLANCHARD, son of Col. Joseph, was born in Dunstable, April 28, 1729. He lived in Dunstable and in Merrimack. Later he resided a few years in Amherst, and about 1800, he removed to Thornton where he owned considerable land. He represented Merrimack in the Provincial assembly 1762-1765, and was a selectman of that town several years. He was a skillful surveyor and he established the bounds of many grants and new townships. He was employed by the Masonian proprietors to run the straight and later the curved line of the Mason patent.

He was associated with Rev. Samuel Langdon, D. D., in the publication in 1761 of the well-known map of New Hampshire.

Gov. Plumer credits the map to Jonathan Blanchard, and many have assumed that it was Col. Joseph Blanchard, the father, who died in 1758, who was the associate of Rev. Dr. Langdon.

The map bears a dedicatory inscription as follows:

To the Right Honorable Charles Townsend, His Majesty's Secretary at War, & One of His Majesty's most Honorable Privy Council &c. this Map of the Province of New Hampshire Is Humbly Inscribed by

His most Obliged &
Most Obed^t Serv^{ts}.
JOSEPH BLANCHARD.
SAMUEL LANGDON.

Col. Joseph Blanchard married in Westford, September 19, 1748, Betty Spalding, born December 4, 1728, daughter of Joseph and Mary Spalding of Groton and Dunstable. He married, second, Lucy Lovewell, daughter of Col. Zaccheus Lovewell, see. A record of the death of his first wife has not been discovered. The second wife, Lucy, was the mother of seven children.

Thirty Dunstable Families.

i. JOSEPH, born June 21, 1752; died July 10, 1752.

ii. JOSEPH, born May 28, 1753. He lived in Chester. He was a representative 1787-1793, state senator 1794-1799, executive councillor 1800, 1801 and delegate to constitutional conventions. He died March 7, 1833. He married Sarah Calef, born June 12, 1749, daughter of Robert and Hannah (Flanders) Calef of Chester. She died December 2, 1793. He married, second, Mrs. Dorothy (Johnson) Folsom, born, Newbury, Mass., 1747, daughter of Rev. William and Elizabeth (Bradstreet) Johnson and widow of David Folsom. She died May 14, 1836. Eight children: (1) *Joseph*, married Abigail Rogers; (2) *Lucy*, married Thomas Montgomery; (3) *Eleazer*, died unmarried 1809; (4) *Nancy*, died unmarried, 1809; (5) *Sarah*, married Josiah Melvin; (6) *Cyrus*, died unmarried 1809; (7) *Hannah*, married Samuel Dinsmore; (8) *Mary*, married Richard Fitz.

iii. ELEAZER, born June 8, 1755. He was a soldier at Bunker Hill and siege of Boston, 1775.

iv. LUCY, born June, 1757; married Andrew Wilkins, born 1761, son of Rev. Daniel and Sarah (Fuller) Wilkins of Amherst. They removed to Detroit, Michigan. Eight children.

v. CATHERINE, born August 16, 1759, married William Barker of St. John, New Brunswick.

vi. ZACCHEUS, born December 30, 1761. Receipt for wages of Zaccheus Blanchard to May 10, 1783, on the frigate *Hague*, commanded by Capt. J. Manley; receipt signed by Joseph Blanchard, father of said Zaccheus Blanchard. It is probable that Zaccheus died in service, May 10, 1783. See Massachusetts Soldiers and Sailors of the Revolution.

vii. HANNAH, born April 22, 1764, married March 10, 1785, Joseph Nichols, born November 11, 1765, son of Gen. Moses and Hannah (Eaton) Nichols of Amherst. Ten children born in Amherst. They removed, 1811, to Canada.

7. GEN. JONATHAN BLANCHARD, son of Col. Joseph, born September 18, 1738. He lived in Dunstable and was prominent in province and state affairs. He was a delegate to the fifth provincial congress, 1775, and the first house of Representatives, 1776, a councillor, 1776, 1777 and 1778, a member of the State Committee of Safety, from June 13 to December 14, 1777, and from December 20, 1777, to May 20, 1778. He was one of the commissioners from New Hampshire in the convention at New Haven, 1778, to regulate prices and was a delegate in the Continental Congress, 1783, 1784, 1787. He was the first Judge of Probate under the State Constitution of 1783. In military affairs he was a major as early as 1765, and a brigadier general in the

Thirty Dunstable Families. 11

militia 1784-1788. He married Rebecca Farwell, born October 9, 1739, daughter of Oliver and Abigail (Hubbard) Farwell. He died July 16, 1788. His widow, Abigail, died August 12, 1811. They had six children.

- i. REBECCA, born May 4, 1766; married Dr. Ebenezer Starr. See Hannah Blanchard.
- ii. GRACE, born 1768; married December 30, 1790, Frederick French, born September 26, 1766, son of Capt. Benjamin and Molly (Lovewell) French. See French family.
- iii. SOPHIA, married Joseph Farwell, born 1772, son of Oliver and Abigail (Danforth) Farwell of Merrimack.
- iv. ABIGAIL, born November 20, 1770; married December 15, 1797, Dr. Joseph F. Eastman, born January 4, 1772, son of Jonathan and Sarah (Fletcher) Eastman. He was a physician of Hollis. He died September 30, 1865. She died October 7, 1848. Six children.
- v. CHARLES, born March 14, 1776. Harvard University 1796; died at Batavia, New York, March 16, 1811.
- vi. ELIZABETH, married January 7, 1796, Thomas French, born May 7, 1768, son of Capt. Benjamin and Molly (Lovewell) French. Lived at Dunstable. He died May 3, 1846; she died May 4, 1843. See French family.

8. COL. JOTHAM BLANCHARD, son of Col. Joseph, was born in Dunstable 1744 or 1745. He lived in Portsmouth and Peterborough in New Hampshire and after 1785 in Truro, Nova Scotia. A son Jotham is named in the will of Col. Joseph, dated April 6, 1758, and proved May 3, 1758, and in 1765 and 1766, Rebecca, widow of Col. Joseph, conveys land to her son Jotham, a merchant of Portsmouth. While a resident of Portsmouth he was a captain of the Colonial militia. He removed, 1773, to Peterborough, where he was honored by frequent election to office during the Revolution. He was moderator, 1774, 1776, 1777, 1778, 1780, 1781, a selectman 1777, 1778, 1779, 1780, 1781. He was a representative for the year 1778, and was one of the most prominent members of the sessions of that memorable year. March 5, 1778, John Wentworth of Dover, Samuel Cutts of Portsmouth and Jotham Blanchard of Peterborough were appointed a committee to draft an act of prescription and confiscation of the estates of tories. He was one of the Committee of Safety in 1776, and the same year he joined with the patriots of Peterborough in signing the association test pledging property and life in support of the Revolution.

Overlooking his record Sabine includes Jotham

Blanchard in his sketches of the tories of the Revolution, but misstates his residence and erroneously says he "served in a Loyalist corps."

It should also be noted that George King, August 12, 1777, wrote to Meshech Weare: "Mr. Jotham Blanchard of Peterborough has lately purchased in the Eastern Country a quantity of cattle." The writer further says that he is apprehensive that the cattle are intended to feed our enemies. There is no record that the apprehensions of the writer were shared by the government of New Hampshire. At the close of the Revolution there was an animated controversy over the proposed and the adopted measures of organic law, and it is possible that Jotham Blanchard was not in sympathy with the provisions of the state constitution adopted in 1783. His frequent election to office by his townsmen is certain proof that he was not a tory.

He removed in 1785 from Peterborough to Truro, Nova Scotia, where he was successful in business and a colonel of the militia. He died March 18, 1807. He married in Middleton, Mass., November 10, 1766, Elizabeth Treadwell, born 1738 or 1739, died January 5, 1811, daughter of Jacob and Sarah (Cotton) Treadwell of Portsmouth. The officiating minister was Rev. Elias Smith, a brother-in-law of the groom. Four children were born in Portsmouth and five in Peterborough.

    i. JOHN, baptized Portsmouth, March 22, 1767. When the family removed from Peterborough, the children, John, Jonathan and Rebecca were left at Peterborough, probably with Samuel Treadwell, a brother of Mrs. Blanchard. About 1790, John removed from the state and a subsequent record has not been found.

    ii. SARAH, baptized at Portsmouth, November 6, 1768; married at Truro, Jacob Lippincott, a tanner of Truro.

    iii. ELIZABETH, baptized at Portsmouth July 29, 1770; married at Truro, Nathaniel Symonds. They settled at Antigonish, N. S., where she died September 25, 1808.

    iv. REBECCA, baptized at Portsmouth March 1, 1772; married ———— Shepard. She did not remove to Nova Scotia.

    v. HANNAH, born at Peterborough, 1774; married at Truro, 1799, David Archibald, born in Londonderry, N. H., September 27, 1758, son of David and Elizabeth (Elliot) Archibald. He was a shipbuilder, living at Truro and at St. Mary's river. He died 1823; she died 1830.

    vi. JONATHAN, born at Peterborough, April 21, 1776. He lived in Peterborough and vicinity until 1801, when he removed to Truro, removing to Pictou in 1817. He married in

Deering, N. H., December 2, 1798, Sarah Coggin. She died in Pictou, September 25, 1836. Jonathan Blanchard married, second, November 2, 1837, Martha Archibald, daughter of David and Esther (Cox) Archibald. He died May 31, 1843, aged 67 years.

vii. EDWARD SHERBURNE, born at Peterborough, 1778; married at Truro, February 18, 1802, Jane Archibald, daughter of Matthew and Jennet (Fisher) Archibald. He was an innholder, a justice of the peace and commissioner of schools. He died December 24, 1856. His widow died February 9, 1873.

viii. NANCY, born at Peterborough, 1780; married September 2, 1802, Rev. John Waddell, born in Scotland, April 10, 1771. He was a preacher many years in Colchester County, N. S., where he died November 13, 1842. She died August 18, 1818.

ix. JOTHAM, born at Peterborough, 1784. He was an infant when the family removed from Peterborough to Pictou. He was a lawyer and a member of the Parliament of Nova Scotia. He married Widow Margaret Spear, whom he met while traveling in Scotland. He died in Pictou in 1839.

9. AUGUSTUS BLANCHARD, born July 29, 1746, son of Col. Joseph. He was a captain of the six weeks men sent to reinforce the army at Boston, in December, 1775, and in 1776, was commissioned captain in the forces sent to Canada. He lived in Merrimack, Amherst and Milford, and was a valued townsman. He married Bridget Lovewell, daughter of Col. Zacchens Lovewell. See Lovewell family. They had thirteen children.

i. SARAH, born at Dunstable, January 3, 1766; married October 9, 1781, John Stearns, born April 25, 1755, son of John and Rachel (Codman) Stearns of Amherst. They removed to Vermont.

ii. PRISCILLA, born at Merrimack, August 12, 1768; married John Crosby, born, Milford, April 10, 1768, son of Capt. Josiah and Sarah (Fitch) Crosby. Removed to Maine, engaging in manufacture of lime. He was drowned in Belgrade, Maine, September 20, 1805. Six children. She married, second, Solomon Hallett. She died 1847.

iii. AUGUSTUS, born January 18, 1770; married January 31, 1793, Esther Crosby, born in Milford, February 3, 1771, daughter of Capt. Josiah and Sarah (Fitch) Crosby. He was a clothier in Hopkinton and Sandwich, New Hampshire. He died October 11, 1829. She died January 20, 1849. Seven children.

iv. HANNAH, born February 27, 1772; married Joel Crosby, born in Lexington, February 9, 1763, son of Samson and Lucy (Richardson) Crosby of Lexington and Amherst. He was a soldier in the Revolution with a good record. He died in Leominster, Mass., October 20, 1833. She died February 19, 1846.

v. ESTHER, born May 4, 1774; married January 26, 1796, Roger Eliot Perkins, born in Middleton, Massachusetts, July 11, 1769, son of Timothy and Hannah (Trowbridge) Perkins. They lived in Hopkinton, New Hampshire. He owned liberal measures of land and was a useful townsman. He died April 14, 1825. His wife, Esther, died December 8, 1824. They had eight children and are the grandparents of George Hamilton Perkins, Commodore United States Navy.

vi. BRIDGET, born June 23, 1776; married September 23, 1806, Timothy Danforth, born April 2, 1778, son of David and Elizabeth Danforth of Amherst. His second marriage. They lived in Amherst, where she died July 16, 1837. Three children.

vii. REBECCA, born November 18, 1778; married July, 1798, Josiah French, born in Dracut, January 18, 1772, son of Benjamin and Bathsheba (Hill) French of Dracut and Milford. He was a tanner of Milford. He died January 13, 1850; she died March 29, 1850. Twelve children. children.

viii. JAMES, born February 25, 1781; died March 18, 1798.

ix. GEORGE, born August 16, 1783; married Phebe (Lovejoy) Connor. He died 1831.

x. JONATHAN, born November 22, 1785; died September 29, 1788.

xi. PORTER, born August, 16, 1788; married November 4, 1810, Anne Stickney Souther, born, Concord, New Hampshire, February 19, 1791, daughter of John and Mary (Stickney) Souther and granddaughter of Col. Thomas and Anna (Osgood) Stickney of Concord. He was a cabinetmaker of Concord. Later he originated and manufactured the "Blanchard churn" of a liberal celebrity. He died May 25, 1871. Miss Grace Blanchard, librarian of Concord public library is a granddaughter.

xii. JONATHAN, born April 9, 1793; no record secured.

xiii. CATHERINE, born July 18, 1796; married 1830, Rufus Taylor. Lived in Damariscotta, Maine.

1. ANDREW COOKE came to Dunstable about 1680. He owned land and built a house near the Lovewell homestead. He was chosen a fence viewer in 1683 and during the ensuing ten years he is frequently mentioned in the records. He married Phebe Lovewell, a daughter of John Lovewell, senior, and an aunt of Capt. John Lovewell. The record of their marriage is in Chelmsford. "Andrew Cooke married July 24, 1685, Phebe, daughter of John Loven both of Dunstable." About 1693, and during King William's War, he removed with Joseph Lovewell to the part of Watertown now Weston, Mass. His wife, Phebe, was admitted to the

church of Weston, November 3, 1717. He died in Weston, February 1, 1717-8.

Children of Andrew and Phebe (Lovewell) Cooke:

- i. LYDIA, born in Dunstable, July 26, 1686.
2. ii. ANDREW, born in Dunstable, November 10, 1687.
- iii. ELIZABETH, born in Dunstable, March 18, 1689; married October 17, 1705, John Wadkins.
- iv. ALICE, born in Dunstable, October 7, 1690; married May 24, 1723, Theophilus Phillips, born June 24, 1688, son of Theophilus and Mary (Bennett) Phillips; removed to Hopkinton, Mass.
- v. PHEBE, born about 1794; married February 16, 1717-8, Nathaniel Morse, son of Dea. John and Abigail (Stearns) Morse. Both owned the covenant in the church of Weston in July, 1719. They had three or more children. He died March 10, 1729-30.
3. vi JOSEPH, born about 1698.
- vii. JOHN, a minor 1718.
- viii. THOMAS, a minor 1718.

2. ANDREW COOKE, son of Andrew and Phebe (Lovewell) Cooke, was born in Dunstable, November 10, 1687. He was a farmer of Weston, where he died 1721. He married in Weston, April 24, 1712, Martha Beale, perhaps his cousin and a daughter of William Beale, see. She died February 4, 1717-8. He married, second, Mary Phillips, born in Watertown, November 15, 1685, daughter of Theophilus and Mary (Bennett) Phillips. One child by first and one by second marriage. Joseph Lovewell, Jr., was appointed guardian of the daughter, Thankful.

- i. THANKFUL, baptized in Weston, August 8, 1714.
- ii. MARY, born April 6, 1721.

3. JOSEPH COOKE, son of Andrew and Phebe (Lovewell) Cooke, was very probably born in Watertown, now Weston, about 1698. He married November 10, 1726, Mindwell Hyde, born April 5, 1703, daughter of Eleazer and Hannah (Hyde) Hyde of Newton, Mass. He lived in Newton, and there died January 11, 1749. His widow died February 13, 1786.

- i. JOSEPH, born August 26, 1729; died August 4, 1730.
- ii. JOSIAH, born September 9, 1731; married April 26, 1753, Mary Oldham.

iii. HANNAH, born March 5, 1733, died December 31, 1748.
iv. OLIVER, born June 1, 1735, married January 20, 1757, Huldah Knapp.
v. SOLOMON, born July 16, 1738.
vi. THOMAS, born May 17, 1740.

1. JOHN CROMWELL. Of this pioneer of the Merrimack Valley in New Hampshire, there are many conflicting statements and much has been written of him which is not supported by the records of his time. Omitting the fanciful coloring of tradition and the stories of buried treasure, the record of John Cromwell is a simple narrative of a man of adventure and courage, living without the support of community and braving the danger of an exposed frontier. He removed before 1656, from Charlestown, where he had lived several years, to the west bank of the Merrimack river in the present town of Merrimack. Here he built a house and established trade with the Indians, receiving furs in exchange for blankets and rum. The location of his house is established by contemporaneous records. In 1656, the General Court of Massachusetts made a grant of 8000 acres to the town of Billerica, which was located on both sides of the Merrimack river. On the original map or plan of this grant, made by Jonathan Danforth in 1656, "Cromwell house" is located on the west bank of the Merrimack river at a point south of Thornton's Ferry. See N. H. State Papers, Vol. XXIV., page 166. The grant was sold by John Parker, agent for Billerica, to William Brenton and subsequently was known as Brenton Farm. In the conveyance to Mr. Brenton "the trucking house now inhabited by John Cromwell" is noted. See Suffolk Registry, Liber III., page 186. The record cited is proof that Cromwell in 1656 had built a house within the limits of Brenton Farm. Having no title to the premises, he was a squatter there. The statement that he was driven away by the Indians in a time of peace is tradition and it is more probable that William Brenton was the compulsive influence which urged his removal. In the autumn of 1659, or early in 1660, he purchased of Dea. Edward Johnson of Woburn, a grant of 300 acres situated in the part of Dunstable now Tyngsborough. Here he built a mansion house and made substantial improvements upon the land. He died in 1661. The appraisal of his estate is dated November 28, 1661, and was returned by

John Parker, Jacob Parker and William Fletcher. The inventory includes a farm of three hundred acres, a mansion house and out buildings, clothing, furniture, farming implements, twenty cattle and horses, twelve swine, a quantity of furs and goods for trade with the Indians. The total value is £608 2s 8d. The widow, Seaborne Cromwell, conveyed the land and buildings to John Hull of Boston, January 22, 1662-3. Mr. Hull sold the premises to Lieut. Joseph Wheeler, January 29, 1676-7. At this house the proprietors held their first meetings in Dunstable. To amend some defect in the title in 1702, John Cromwell of Andover and Benjamin Cromwell of Woodbridge, East Jersey, sons of John Cromwell, late of the trading house, merchant, and Robert Cumbey of Boston and Rebecca, his wife, daughter of said John Cromwell give a quitclaim to Peter Bulkeley, Esq., of Concord. Later Col. Ebenezer Bancroft owned and occupied a part of the premises many years.

John Cromwell married Seaborn Bachelder, who was baptized in Charlestown, March 12, 1634-5, a daughter of William and Jane (Cowper) Bachelder. He died 1661. She married, second, May 22, 1663, Robert Parris, see. In 1670, one son was deceased and two sons and a daughter were living in Charlestown, in the home of their grandfather, William Bachelder.

 i. JOHN, probably not married; he was killed by accident in Andover, Mass., September 20, 1708. "Simply and un- advisedly acting the Gesture of ye Indian Enemy was shot to death in the woods supposing him to be one of our enemys."

 ii. BENJAMIN, lived in Woodbridge, New Jersey. He married in Charlestown, March 5, 1702-3, Mary Patten of Woburn.

 iii. JOSEPH, died young.

 iv. REBECCA, married Robert Cumbey, born in Boston, February 14, 1654, son of Humphrey and Sarah Cumbey. They lived in Boston, where four children were born.

1. JOHN DARBYSHIRE came to Dunstable about 1695. He could not write and the clerks transcribed his name in many forms, of which Darbyshire, Derbyshire and Darbyshear are the more common. In one instance the name is written Derby. It is said that his descendants abbreviated the name and are mingled with the more numerous family of Derby. He married Mary Blanchard, daughter of Dea. John Blanchard. See

Blanchard family. He removed, about 1704, from Dunstable to Groton, where he resided several years. He died before 1725. June 5, 1725, county records, September 14, 1725, church records, Nathaniel Woods of Groton married Widow Mary Darbyshire. He was a son of Samuel and Alice (Rushton) Woods and she was his fourth wife. Both died at Groton. Four children of John and Mary (Blanchard) Darbyshire:

    i. WILLIAM, born Dunstable, August 14, 1698.
    ii. JAMES, born Dunstable, April 30, 1702.
    iii. MARY, born Groton, January 3, 1705-6.
    iv. OLIVER, born Groton, December 8, 1708.

1. SAMUEL FRENCH, son of Lieut. William and Elizabeth French of Cambridge and Billerica, was born in Billerica about 1660. In several printed records the date of his birth is December 3, 1645. The son, Samuel, born on that date, died in Cambridge, July 15, 1646. The date of the birth of the second Samuel is not of record. He removed to Dunstable about 1680, and married in Chelmsford, December 28, 1682, Sarah Cummings, born January 28, 1661, daughter of John and Sarah (Howlet) Cummings. He lived east of Nutting Hill. He was one of the foundation members of the church, a selectman and an honored citizen. He died November 17, 1757. Eight children.

    i. SARAH, born February 7, 1683-4.
    ii. SAMUEL, born September 10, 1685; if he was married, a record has not been found. He died November 4, 1727.
2. iii. JOSEPH, born March 10, 1687-8.
3. iv. JOHN, born May 6, 1691.
    v. EBENEZER, born April 7, 1693; he was killed by the Indians, September 5, 1724. His wife was Esther. Their son, EBENEZER, was born in Dunstable, October 27, 1723.
    vi. RICHARD, born April 8, 1695.
    vii. ALICE, born November 20, 1699; married after 1719, Nathaniel Woods, born in Groton, October 19, 1694, son of Nathaniel Woods. He was a sergeant in Lovewell's third expedition and on the day of the battle was in command of the fort. They lived in Groton.
    viii. JONATHAN, born February 1, 1703-4. He married Jane ———. He died November 17, 1757. In his will there is no mention of children. He left his property to Oliver Woods, a son of his sister Alice.

Thirty Dunstable Families. 19

2. JOSEPH FRENCH, son of Samuel, born March 10, 1687-8; married Elizabeth Cummings, born January 5, 1687-8, a daughter of John, Jr., and Elizabeth (Kinsley) Cummings. He was a captain and a selectman. His wife, Elizabeth, died April 30, 1751. Eight children.

- 4. i. JOSEPH, born July 28, 1713.
- ii. ELIZABETH, born 1715; married 1736, Capt. John Cummings, born January 14, 1698, son of Nathaniel and Abigail (Parkhurst) Cummings. Lived in Dunstable. He died August 15, 1770. She died July 2, 1793. Eight children.
- iii. SAMSON, born July 28, 1717; he removed to Southwick, Mass. He was twice married and had sons, Samson, Jonathan, David, Aaron and Daniel.
- iv. JOSIAH, born February 24, 1722-3.
- v. THOMAS, born June 29, 1724.
- 5. vi. BENJAMIN, born July 6, 1726.
- vii. SAMUEL, born July 14, 1728.
- viii. SAMUEL, born August 10, 1730.

3. JOHN FRENCH, son of Samuel, born May 6, 1691. He bought land of his father, 1714, of Henry Farwell, 1721, and a part of the Brattle farm, 1732. He was a farmer and a wheelwright. He lived in the part of original Dunstable now Dunstable, Mass.

- i. JOHN, born March 1, 1719.
- ii. WILLIAM, born October 18, 1721.
- iii. HANNAH, born January 24, 1723-4.
- iv. ELEAZER, born October 12, 1726.
- v. ELIZABETH, born April 29, 1729.
- vi. EBENEZER, born May 31, 1731.
- vii. SARAH, born October 6, 1733.

4. JOSEPH FRENCH, son of Joseph, born July 28, 1713. He was prominent in civil and military affairs, a town officer and colonel in the militia. His first wife, Bridget, died October 29, 1735, his second wife, Elizabeth, died January 20, 1753, and his third wife, Rebecca, died March 21, 1776. Eight children.

- i. ISAAC, born May 26, 1734; died August 4, 1753.
- 6. ii. JOSEPH born November 1, 1739.
- iii. JOSIAH, born June 27, 1741; died young.
- iv. JOSIAH, born June 17, 1743.

Thirty Dunstable Families.

- v. THOMAS, born May 4, 1745.
- vi. ELIZABETH, born March 6, 1746-7.
- vii. BRIDGET, born August 30, 1749.
- viii. MOLLIE, twin, born August 30, 1749.
- ix. SUSANNAH, born October 16, 1757.
- 7. x. THEODORE, born June 6, 1759.

5. BENJAMIN FRENCH, son of Joseph, born July 6, 1726. He was a town officer, representative and a captain. He married January 8, 1751, Molly Lovewell, born May 26, 1732, daughter of Col. Zaccheus Lovewell, see. She died December 17, 1774. He married, second, February 1, 1776, Mary Cummings, widow of Jeremiah Cummings. He died December 15, 1779.

- i. BENJAMIN, born December 4, 1752; died October 29, 1776.
- ii. ESTHER, born January 7, 1754; married Dr. Allin Toothaker, second, Timothy Taylor, Esq. See Taylor family.
- iii. MOLLIE, born October 18, 1756.
- iv. KATHERINE, born August 19, 1758.
- v. AUGUSTUS, born June 16, 1760.
- vi. BETSEY, born January 16, 1762.
- vii. CHARLOTTE, born September 21, 1763; married July 12, 1779, James Cummings, born, Dunstable, July 12, 1757, son of Oliver and Sybel (Bailey) Cummings. Lived in Dunstable. He died September 6, 1840; she died September 27, 1787. Four children.
- viii. FREDERICK, born September 26, 1766; he was one of the foremost citizens of Dunstable many years. Representative, 1793, 1795, 1797, 1803, 1805 and 1806. He was appointed a justice of the peace, February 15, 1791, and his commissions were renewed until his death. About 1810 he was appointed clerk of the court of Hillsborough county, and removed to Amherst. He died March 28, 1824. He married December 30, 1790, Grace Blanchard, daughter of Gen. Jonathan Blanchard, see. She died in Lowell, February 6, 1845. They had five children. Among these was *Benjamin Franklin French*, born in Dunstable, October 2, 1791, Dartmouth College, 1812. He was an able lawyer of Nashua, and subsequently the masterly agent of the Jackson Corporation. He died in Lowell, May 16, 1853.
- ix. THOMAS, born August 7, 1768; he was an active and able man, a town officer and representative. He married January 7, 1796, Elizabeth Blanchard, daughter of Gen. Jonathan Blanchard, see. He died May 3, 1846; she died May 4, 1843.
- x. LUCY, born November 7, 1769.
- xi. BRIDGET, born January 14, 1772.

Thirty Dunstable Families. 21

6. JOSEPH FRENCH, son of Joseph, born November 1, 1739, He was a man of ability and a prominent citizen of Dunstable. He married March 3, 1768, Sybel Richardson, born in Chelmsford, May 19, 1744, daughter of John and Esther Richardson. Four children.
   i. ELIZABETH, born October 7, 1769.
   ii. ISAAC, born March 28, 1771.
   iii. SYBEL, born December 12, 1773.
   iv. MARY, born June 4, 1776.

7. THEODORE FRENCH, son of Joseph, born June 6, 1759. Lived in Dunstable. He was a representative 1801 and 1804. He married October 4, 1781, Rhoda Danforth, born in Dunstable, April 22, 1769, daughter of Lieut. Josiah and Mary (Richardson) Danforth. She died May 20, 1790. He married, second, February 3, 1791, Caty (Honey) Lovewell, born in Dunstable, March 2, 1759, daughter of John Honey and widow of Jonathan Lovewell, Jr., see. Five children of the first and three of the second wife.
   i. RHODA, born July 9, 1782.
   ii. JOSEPH, born November 22, 1783.
   iii. REBECCA, born June 4, 1785.
   iv. THEODORE, born December 19, 1786; lived in Concord. He was agent for the Boston and Concord Boating Company and the first freight agent of the Concord railroad.
   v. JACOB, born October 24, 1789; died April 15, 1790.
   vi. KATEY, born September 1, 1792.
   vii. JOHN L., born June 5, 1795.
   viii. JOHN F., born January 21, 1798.

1. DANIEL GALUSHA, the ancestor of a numerous family in Massachusetts and Vermont, was a soldier in King Philip's War. In the summer of 1676, he was one of the men posted at the garrison in Springfield. In this war many of the soldiers assigned their pay to the towns from which they enlisted. Daniel Galusha assigned his pay to the town of Reading. It is not known when he came to America or where he had lived previous to his service in the war. When discharged at Springfield, he repaired to Chelmsford and there married October 10, 1676, Hannah Goold, born July 18, 1655, daughter of Francis and Rose Goold of Chelmsford and a sister of Samuel and John Goold of Dunstable.

He lived in Chelmsford about twenty years and there seven children were born. There is no record of his death in Chelmsford but the record of birth of the youngest child is in these words: Richard, son of Widow Galusha, was born December 4, 1696.

The family removed from Chelmsford to Dunstable soon after 1696, and lived near Salmon brook. In Queen Anne's War the house of the Galusha family was one of the fortified garrisons. The Indians made an attack upon the house July 3, 1706. The house was burned, and the daughter, Rachel, was slain. Both Penhallow and Pike, who were contemporaneous writers make mention of the event. In the journal of Rev. John Pike, the story is briefly told. "Near about the same time, or soon after, they assalted another house belonging to one Jacob Guletia, a Dutchman. The house was burnt, some persons were killed and some escaped."

Penhallow in "Narrative of the Indian Wars" written at the time and printed in 1726, says: "After that a small party attacked Daniel Galeutia's house, who held them play for some time, till the old man's courage failed; when on surrendering himself, he informed them of the state of the garrison, how that one man was killed and only two men and a boy left, which caused them to rally anew, and with greater courage than before. Upon which one with the boy got out on the back side, leaving only Jacob to fight the battle, who for some time defended himself with much bravery; but overpowered with force, and finding none to assist him, was obliged to quit and make his escape as well as he could; but before he got far, the enemy laid hold of him once and again, and yet with much struggling he escaped himself. Upon this they burnt the house."

In this narrative Penhallow mentions Daniel Galusha calling him an old man in specific terms that challenges the accuracy of the Chelmsford records, which mentions widow Galusha in 1696. That Daniel Galusha, the father, was living in 1706 is confirmed by the testimony of one of his sons. In 1712, Daniel Galusha, born in 1686, petitioned the General Court concerning a gun, the value of which had been deducted from his wages on the pay roll in 1706. He recites: "About six years past, when the Indians attacked and took the house of Daniel Galusha, his father, in Dunstable, he being posted there under her Majesty's pay, and serving there with his own arms, while running hastily to take his own gun, by mistake he took one of the public arms, and the enemy pressing sore upon him, he was forced to make his escape, the house being burned by the enemy, with his gun and others therein." The date of the death of Daniel Galusha, the father, is not known. It was before 1713, when widow Hannah Galusha removed from Brookline to the home of her son in Weston. It will be observed that Pike calls Mr. Galusha a Dutchman, and in the Court Records of Massachusetts he is so designated. It is a tradition among his descendants that he was a native of Wales. After the destruction of their home in Dunstable, the widow, Hannah, lived a short time in Brookline, removing to the home of her son, Daniel, in 1714. There were seven children of Daniel and Hannah (Goold) Galusha, born in Chelmsford.

  i. HANNAH, born September 10, 1677.

  ii. JACOB, born April 22, 1680. He was a soldier in Queen Anne's War and the brave defender of the Galusha garrison in 1706. It is possible that he was the ancestor of the many families of the name in Rehoboth, Norton, Lynn and Danvers.

  iii. RACHEL, born July 18, 1683, was killed by the Indians July 3, 1706.

2. iv. DANIEL, born March 31, 1686.

3. v. NATHANIEL, born December 22, 1691.

  vi. DINAH, born January 14, 1695.

  vii. RICHARD, born December 4, 1696.

2. DANIEL GALUSHA, son of Daniel, born in Chelmsford, March 31, 1686. He was a soldier in 1702 and 1706, and probably other dates during Queen Anne's War. Soon after the destruction of his home in Dunstable, he removed to the west precinct of Watertown, now Weston. He was a carpenter and a farmer and the owner of considerable land in Weston. In 1716 he removed to Colchester, Connecticut, and was there admitted an inhabitant, December 22, 1718. He married in Watertown, July 5, 1710, Sarah Warren, a daughter of Daniel and Elizabeth (Whitney) Warren of Watertown. Five children.

  i. DANIEL, born in Weston, May 9, 1711; died young.

  ii. DINAH, born in Weston, April, 1713.

  iii. DANIEL, born in Weston, April 26, 1716.

  iv. ELIZABETH, born in Colchester, October 3, 1719.
4. v. JACOB, born in Colchester, about 1721.

3. NATHANIEL GALUSHA, son of Daniel, born in Chelmsford, December 22, 1691. His wife was Anna. He was of Sudbury, 1714-1716, and subsequently he lived a few years in Rutland, Mass. No later record is found. It is probable he was the ancestor of the families of Galusha in Williamstown, West Stockbridge and southern Vermont. The record of birth of three children is given.

  i. JACOB, born Sudbury, May 7, 1715.

  ii. NATHANIEL, born Rutland, December 16, 1719.

  iii. RACHEL, born Rutland, December 27, 1720.

4. JACOB GALUSHA, son of Daniel, was born in Colchester, Conn., about 1721. He lived in Norwich, Conn., until 1769, when he removed to Salisbury, Conn. From Salisbury, he removed to Shaftsbury, Vermont, in 1775 or 1776. The record of his time affords frequent evidence of his fortitude and ability. Several of his sons were officers in the Revolution and the name enlivens the annals of Vermont. He married in Norwich, September 10, 1745, Lydia Huntington, a daughter of Matthew and Lydia (Leonard) Huntington. She died in Norwich, May 6, 1764. He married, second, September 9, 9, 1764, Thankful ———. He married, third, Desire Andrus) Metcalf, who died in Salisbury, September 28, 1775. He married, fourth, Abigail Porter of Norwich. Nine children by first, one by second, and six by third wife.

  i. MARY, born November 10, 1746.

  ii. DAVID, born October 30, 1748; married January 31, 1773, Charity Luther. She died April 15, 1777. He married, second, November 21, 1779, Rhoda ———.

  iii. JACOB, born December 28, 1750; married February 13, 1765, Parthania Ward. He lived in Shaftsbury. He died July 25, 1834; his widow died August 13, 1846.

  iv. JONAS, born February 4, 1753. He lived in Shaftsbury and was constantly employed in public affairs. He was a sheriff, councillor, judge of the county court, presidential elector, and governor of Vermont 1809 to 1819, except 1813 and 1814. He married Mary Chittenden, a daughter of Gov. Thomas and Elizabeth (Meigs) Chittenden. She died April 20, 1794. He married, second, Martha Sammons, who died November 10, 1797; he married, third,

Thirty Dunstable Families. 25

June 30, 1808, Abigail Ward, who died May 6, 1809; he married, fourth, Abigail (Atwater) Beach, who died July 30, 1831. He died September 25, 1834.

v. AMOS, born April 1, 1755, died in Shaftsbury, October 16, 1839. His wife, Mary, died July 3, 1819.

vi. ELIJAH, born October 23, 1757; married Beulah Chittenden, a daughter of Gov. Thomas and Elizabeth (Meigs) Chittenden. He died a few years later. His widow married, second, Col. Matthew Lyon, a native of Ireland, who lived several years in Fairhaven, Vermont, and later in Kentucky and Arkansas. He was a member of Congress from Vermont and Kentucky, and a delegate from the territory of Arkansas. He died August 1, 1822. His widow died 1824, near Little Rock, Arkansas. The story of his career is one of romantic incident and of unusual interest. His sons were able and brilliant men.

vii. OLIVE, born December 4, 1759.

viii. LYDIA, born June 1, 1762; married in Salisbury, October 19, 1786, Asa Hutchinson.

ix. ANNA, born May 6, 1764; married in Salisbury, Ebenezer Wright, born April 10, 1765, son of Amaziah and Zerviah (Fitch) Wright of Mansfield, Conn.

x. LUCY, born May 5, 1765.

xi. DANIEL.

xii. BENJAMIN.

xiii. EZRA.

xiv. DESIRE, born, Salisbury, December 31, 1771.

xv. SARAH, born, Salisbury, June 30, 1774.

xvi. ELIAS, born, Salisbury, September 9, 1775. Susannah, daughter of Elias and Susannah Galusha, was born in Salisbury, October 25, 1797.

GOULD. Francis and Rose Goold, immigrant ancestors of one branch of the Gould families of Massachusetts lived in Duxbury, Braintree and Chelmsford. In early records the name appears as Gold, Goold and Gould. Of the twelve children of Francis and Rose Gould, two sons, Samuel and John, and a daughter, Hannah, the wife of Daniel Galusha, have lived in Dunstable.

1. SAMUEL GOULD, son of Francis and Rose, was born in Braintree, August 12, 1658. He came from Chelmsford to Dunstable, 1680. He married at Chelmsford, March 17, 1684, Mehitable Barrett, born April 12, 1665, daughter of Thomas and Frances (Woolderson) Barrett. She was a sister of the wife of John Swallow. He was chosen "dog whipper for the meeting house" May 21,

1688, and his name is found in the records from time to time about twenty years. He returned to Chelmsford, probably soon after 1700, and there died October 27, 1747. His wife died October 3, 1733. The record of birth of the daughter, Margaret, is at Dunstable. The record of birth of the younger children is at Chelmsford. In addition to the eight children named, it is believed by many that there was a son, Joseph, born perhaps in 1697.

    i. MARGARET, born May 26, 1687; married March 30, 1709-10, John Chamberlain, Jr., of Billerica.
    ii. ANNA, born September 12, 1689.
2. iii. SAMUEL, born November 10, 1691.
    iv. JOHN, born January 24, 1693.
    v. JEMIMA, born June 30, 1696.
    vi. MOSES, born March 6, 1699.
    vii. ISAAC, twin, born March 6, 1699.

2. SAMUEL GOULD, son of Samuel, born in Dunstable, November 10, 1691; married in Wenham, July 28, 1720, Mary Batchelder, daughter of Joseph and Sarah Batchelder. He settled in Dunstable previous to his marriage. He bought of Col. Jonathan Tyng, one hundred acres of land. This farm with later additions was partly in Hudson and Pelham, but mainly in the part of Dunstable now Tyngsborough. He is styled Capt. Samuel Gould in the records. His wife died November 26, 1761. He died January 13, 1769. His will was proved January 31, 1775.

    i. JOSEPH, born August 19, 1720; married June 19, 1746, Mary Piper. He lived in Hudson.
    ii. SAMUEL, born January 2, 1723; married January 10, 1750-1, Elizabeth Marble. He died in Tyngsborough, April 2, 1769.
    iii. MARY, born January 24, 1727; married Solomon Pollard.
    iv. MARK, born March 17, 1729; married Abigail Wyman.
    v. SILAS, born September 16, 1733; died January 9, 1756.

3. JOHN GOULD, son of Francis and Rose Gould, was born in Chelmsford, August 21, 1660. He came to Dunstable with his brother, Samuel, in 1680. He married July 2, 1686, Elizabeth Cummings. He died at Dunstable, April 16, 1689. One child.

    i. ELIZABETH, born May 8, 1687.

1. WILLIAM HARWOOD, son of Nathaniel and Elizabeth Harwood, was born in Boston, March 28, 1665. In his infancy the family removed to Concord, where Nathaniel, the father, died February 7, 1715-6. William, the son, married at Concord, May 11, 1692, Esther Perry, born August 11, 1674, daughter of Obadiah and Esther (Hassell) Perry, see. About 1700, they removed to Dunstable. He was a worthy man and a valued citizen. He was elected to office on many occasions. He died September 17, 1740. Esther, his wife, died October 8, 1747. Gravestones. Three children were born at Concord, and seven at Dunstable.

   i. ELIZABETH, born July 1694.
   ii. ESTHER, born January 10, 1696-7; married in Concord, August 26, 1724, Joseph Baker of Marlboro.
   iii. JOHN, born May 28, 1699. He was a soldier in Lovewell's third expedition and was killed at Pigwacket, May 8, 1725.
   iv. THOMAS, born January 9, 1702. He was a prominent citizen.
   v. SARAH, born June 26, 1706; married Dea. William Cummings, son of John and Elizabeth (Kinsley) Cummings. He marched in the third expedition under Capt. John Lovewell; was sent home on account of wounds previously received. He lived in Hudson, where he died August 29, 1757. She died in 1769. They had seven children.
   vi. MARY, born March 25, 1709; married Thomas Pollard of Dunstable. He was a son of Thomas and Sarah (Farmer) Pollard of Billerica.
   vii. ABIGAIL, born April 9, 1710.
   viii. RACHEL, born July 21, 1712.
   ix. DORCAS, born March 6, 1717; died December 11, 1723.
   x. LYDIA, born October 5, 1722.

1. JAMES HARWOOD, son of James and Lydia (Barrett) Harwood of Chelmsford and grandson of Andrew and Elizabeth Harwood of Boston, was born in Chelmsford, September 30, 1695. He lived in Littleton, Concord, and Groton, removing to Dunstable soon after 1740. In the controversy over the settlement of Rev. Samuel Bird, a new light, in 1747, he joined with the Blanchard party in opposing, and against the Lovewell party, who were supporters of Mr. Bird. His wife was Lydia. There is no record of his death and I find no mention of his name after 1754, but his son James wrote his name James Harwood, Junior, as late as 1762.

i. ANDREW, born at Littleton, July 5, 1722.
ii. EUNICE, born at Littleton, March 21, 1724.
iii. MARY, born at Littleton, June 6, 1726.
2. iv. JAMES, born 1737.

2. JAMES HARWOOD, son of James and Lydia Harwood was born at Groton or Concord 1737. His parents removed in his infancy to Dunstable. In the French and Indian War he served in Capt. James Todd's company of Col. Peter Gilman's regiment at Albany, New York, in 1755; in the famous company of rangers under Capt. James Rogers in 1756; in Capt. Nehemiah Lovewell's company of Col. John Goffe's regiment at Crown Point in 1760. In the Revolution he served in Capt. William Walker's company of Col. James Reed's regiment at Bunker Hill and siege of Boston, 1775; in Capt. Daniel Wilkin's company of Col. Timothy Bedel's regiment in Canada, 1776, and in April, 1777, he enlisted into the Continental service for three years. He was assigned to Capt. Amos Emerson's company of Col. Joseph Cilley's regiment. In descriptive list he was 40 years of age, six feet, complexion, hair and eyes, dark. He died of disease, December 1, 1777. He married Mary Clogston, daughter of John and Miranda (Glasford) Clogston of Boston and Dunstable. She married, second, at Dunstable, November 9, 1785, Isaac Foot.

i. JOHN, born 1758. He was a soldier in the Revolution and was wounded at Stillwater, 1777. He married January 9, 1787, Sarah Martin. He lived in Goffstown and Manchester, N. H. He died 1833. From March 1, 1823, he was a pensioner.
ii. JAMES, born 1760. He was a soldier in the Revolution. He died in Unity, N. H., 1800. He married in Billerica, December 4, 1783, Patty Sanders, born October 28, 1759, daughter of David and Abigail (Snow) Sanders.
iii. ARCHIBALD, born 1762. He was a soldier in the Revolution, serving in Capt. William Barron's company of Col. Moses Nichols' regiment, 1780, and in Capt. John Mills' company of Col. Daniel Reynolds' regiment, 1781. Subsequently he lived in Springfield, Weathersfield and Eden, Vt. He was a carpenter and millwright. He married May 8, 1786, Susannah House, daughter of Combs and Prudence House of Springfield, Vt. He died 1837. His widow died 1848. Among his many descendants is Watson H. Harwood, M. D., of Chasm Falls, New York, the genealogist of the family.
iv. ROXANNA, married John Burlingame of Weathersfield, Vt.

Thirty Dunstable Families. 29

    v. LYDIA, married Jonathan Ordway; married, second, Jedediah Hutchins.

1. RICHARD HASSELL, born 1622, settled in Cambridge, before 1643. He was admitted freeman, 1647. He and his wife, Joan, were early members of the church of Cambridge. In the division of Shawshin, now Billerica, by Cambridge in 1652, he received lot 69, of 60 acres. He removed to Billerica in 1676, and April 12, 1678, he was chosen "to inspect the lads on the Sabbath days." He removed from Billerica to Dunstable in 1679. He was an intelligent man and a worthy citizen. There is no record of his death.

        i. ELIZABETH, born September 20, 1643; married November 1, 1661, Joseph Wright, born in Woburn about 1639, son of Dea. John and Priscilla Wright. He was a deacon and a selectman of Woburn. He died March 31, 1724; she died June 28, 1713. Eleven children.

2.   ii. JOSEPH, born September 20, 1645.

      iii. ESTHER, born December 6, 1648; married Obadiah Perry; married, second, Martin Townsend. See Perry family.

      iv. ALICE, born about 1665, married Christopher Temple; married, second, Jacob Kendall. See Temple family.

2. JOSEPH HASSELL, son of Richard, was born in Cambridge, September 20, 1645. He married August 21, 1667, Anna Perry, a daughter of William and Anna Perry of Watertown. In his life he was a good townsman and in the achievement of his descendants his name is boldly written in the annals of Dunstable. His daughter, Anna, was the mother of Capt. John Lovewell, his daughter, Abiah, was the mother of Col. Joseph Blanchard, and his granddaughter, Esther, was the wife of Col. Zaccheus Lovewell. Fox confuses this family with that of Richard, his father. Joseph Hassell and his wife and son, Benjamin, were slain by the Indians, September 2, 1691.

       i. ANNA, born in Watertown, October 6, 1669; married December 7, 1686, John Lovewell. See Lovewell family.

      ii. ELIZABETH, born in Concord, September 11, 1671; died June 19, 1672.

     iii. ABIAH, born in Concord, May 13, 1673; married May 25, 1696, Capt. Joseph Blanchard. See Blanchard family.

3.   iv. JOSEPH, no record of birth.

v. RICHARD was captured by the Indians during Queen Anne's War.
  vi. BENJAMIN was slain by the Indians September 2, 1691.

3. JOSEPH HASSELL, son of Joseph, was born about 1675. He was a soldier, 1702, in the company commanded by Lieut. William Tyng. He lived in Dunstable and the name of his wife was Hannah, but there is no record of his marriage or death. They had one son and seven daughters.

4. i. BENJAMIN, born August 9, 1701.
   ii. HANNAH, born September 10, 1705.
   iii. RACHEL, born March 3, 1707.
   iv. ESTHER, born July 30, 1709; married Col. Zaccheus Lovewell, see.
   v. DINAH, born January 6, 1713.
   vi. ABIAH, born March 16, 1715.
   vii. BETSEY, born August 16, 1718; married November 27, 1740, Robert Pomroy.
   viii. SARAH, born August 4, 1721.

4. BENJAMIN HASSELL, son of Joseph, born in Dunstable, August 9, 1701. He was a soldier in the third expedition of Capt. John Lovewell, and was present at the beginning of the fight at Pigwacket. During the battle he left the field and returned to the fort. At the time he was censured, and he was the soldier whom Rev. Thomas Symmes in his sermon refused to mention by name. Subsequently he was a useful and respected citizen of Merrimack. His daughter, Adah, was the first white child born in that town. Two of his sons served in the Revolution. He married December 18, 1728, Elizabeth Taylor, daughter of John Taylor, see. A record of seven children is found.

   i. ADAH, born April 27, 1734.
5. ii. ELIAS, born June 25, 1740.
   iii. ABEL. He served in the Revolution in Capt Jason Ford's company of Col. Moses Nichols' regiment at Bennington, 1777. He married September 22, 1773, Rachel Houstan and lived in Merrimack. His children were Amos, Hannah and Rachel, who married James Cash.
   iv. KEZIA, born May 7, 1746.
6. v. JASON, born December 4, 1748.
   vi. DEBORAH, born December 7, 1751.
   vii. BENJAMIN, born February 12, 1755.

5. ELIAS HASSELL, son of Benjamin, born June 25, 1740. He settled in Deering. He was a selectman and in 1776 was one of the signers of the association test. He married December 21, 1792, Mary Morrill and removed to Hillsborough. Two children.

    i. HANNAH, born October 2, 1793; married Samuel Morrill. Lived in Deering.

    ii. WILLIAM, born 1799. He lived in Pepperell, Mass., and in New Ipswich, where he died March 3, 1874. He was a deacon of the Congregational church of New Ipswich. He married in Pepperell, November 30, 1826, Betsey H. Butterfield, born in Pepperell, August 9, 1806, daughter of Daniel and Sarah (Shattuck) Butterfield. She died September 21, 1868. He married, second, May 3, 1870, Rhoda (Butterfield) Powers, a sister of his first wife and widow of Nathan Powers of Milford. Three children: *William E.*, born 1823, *James L.*, born 1828 and *George A.*, born 1842, died 1846.

    iii. WILLARD, born in Hillsborough, January 8, 1803. He died unmarried about 1838.

6. JASON HASSELL, son of Benjamin, born December 4, 1748. In the Revolution, he served in Capt. Joseph Moor's company of Col. William Prescott's regiment at Bunker Hill and siege of Boston, 1775. This was a Massachusetts regiment and his name is written Hassell, Harsell and Haskell. In 1778, he was a corporal in Capt. Peter Cross' company of Col. Moses Nichols' regiment which marched to Rhode Island. He was a farmer and lived in Merrimack, where he died 1799. He married December 28, 1779, Elizabeth McClench. Seven children.

    i. ELIZABETH, born November 6, 1785.

    ii. SUKEY, born September 10, 1787.

    iii. LUCY, born September 9, 1789.

    iv. BENJAMIN, born September 19, 1791.

    v. LUTHER RIPLEY, born October 9, 1793.

    vi. JOSEPH, born July 20, 1795.

    vii. CLARISSA, date of birth not on record.

HONEY. This name in early generations was written Behoney. The brothers Gideon, Peter and John, who came to Dunstable, and their descendants have written the name Honey. The daughter, Bridget, in record of her marriage is called Bridget Behoney.

1. PETER BEHONEY, son of Peter and Sarah Behoney was born in Watertown, March 13, 1689-90. He married in Watertown, January 26, 1712-13, Bridget Beale, probably a daughter of Benjamin and Elizabeth (Lovewell) Beale, see. He lived in Watertown, Framingham and Marlborough, Mass. He died in Marlborough, December 13, 1732. The widow and her children removed to Dunstable. It is quite possible that all of the children are not included in this register.

      i. BRIDGET, born about 1714; married in Newbury, Mass., October 16, 1734, Jonathan Lovewell, son of John Lovewell, see.
2.   ii. GIDEON, about 1720.
3.   iii. PETER.
4.   iv. JOHN.

2. GIDEON HONEY, son of Peter, born about 1720, was a minor in 1739. He died in Dunstable, 1757. Administration was granted to his widow, Hannah, June 7, 1757.

      i. HANNAH, born September 20, 1746.
      ii. ELIZABETH, born September 23, 1749.
      iii. WILLIAM, born November 7, 1751.
      iv. BRIDGET, born September 28, 1754.
      v. THIRZAH, born 1756; married Thomas Youngman, son of Nicholas and Mary (Wright) Youngman of Hollis; removed to Washington, Vt.

3. PETER HONEY, son of Peter, lived and probably died in Dunstable. He was a soldier in the Revolution with a good record. There is no record of his marriage. Seven children of Peter and Elizabeth Honey were born in Dunstable.

      i. BRIDGET, born November 7, 1751.
5.   ii. PARMENTER, born August 28, 1753.
      iii. PETER, born January 24, 1756. He was a soldier from Dunstable in the Revolution.
      iv. SARAH, born February 4, 1758; married April 10, 1781, William Elliot of Dunstable.
      v. CALVIN, born July 21, 1762. He was an apprentice of Augustus Blanchard, then of Amherst. He was a soldier in the First Continental Regiment and died in the service 1781.
      vi. ELIZABETH, born 6, 1769.
      vii. LEVINA, born July 26, 1771.

4. JOHN HONEY, son of Peter. He lived in Dunstable and was a soldier in Col. James Reed's regiment. He died in the service, October 24, 1776. His wife was Elizabeth.
   i. KATY, born March 2, 1759; married November 4, 1783, Jonathan Lovewell, see. She married, second, February 3, 1791, Theodore French, see.
   ii. ELIJAH, born July 29, 1764. He lived in Dunstable.
   iii. SHEPARD. There is no record of his birth, but probably he was a son of John and Elizabeth. He lived in Dunstable.

5. PARMENTER HONEY, son of Peter Honey, Jr., was born in Dunstable, August 28, 1753. He was a soldier in the Revolution. He lived in Dunstable, Hollis, and again in Dunstable. He married November 7, 1775, Sarah Hale of Hollis. He married, second, December 22, 1785, Rebecca Snow. His descendants are numerous in Cheshire and Sullivan counties in New Hampshire and in many towns in Vermont.
   i. PARMENTER, born January 30, 1776; married Hannah White. He lived in Lyndeborough and in Acworth, N. H., where he died March 8, 1854. Twelve children.
   ii. SOLOMON.
   iii. CALVIN, married in Watertown, May 5, 1808, Susannah Nutting. Two children born in Watertown, Mass.
   iv. LUTHER, married Betsey Burroughs, daughter of Joseph and Lydia (Preston) Burroughs. Lived in Tyngsborough, Mass.
   v. SARAH.

6. JOSEPH HONEY was a soldier in the Revolution and later had a family and lived in Dunstable. Very probably he was a son of one of the foregoing families.

7. ANN HONEY, of one of the foregoing families, married June 22, 1794, Moses Wentworth, born in Groton or Harvard, 1773, son of Moses and Mindwell (Stone) Wentworth. He died at East Constable, New York, February 5, 1848; she died September 26, 1842. Five children.

1. LOVEWELL. During several years immediately preceding 1665, there were dwelling in Boston two men of the same name, John Lowell; one was a cooper, the other a tanner. This fact is not noted by Savage or in the Lowell Genealogy. John Lowell, the cooper, was

a son of John and a grandson of Percival Lowell. He married, March 3, 1653, Hannah Proctor, who became the mother of John, Mary and Peter, and who was living in 1661. He married, second, probably in 1664, Naomi ———, who was the mother of eleven children. It is currently stated that the second wife was Naomi Sylvester, which is possible but is not proven. Savage and Lowell Genealogy erroneously state that John Lowell, the cooper, married in 1658, Elizabeth Sylvester. This was three or more years before the death of his first wife, Hannah, and both authorities give to John, the cooper, the children of John, the tanner.

John Lowell, the tanner, is the ancestor of the Lovewell family of Dunstable. The date of his arrival in Boston is not definitely known. He was there in 1657, and January 24, 1658, he married in Scituate, Elizabeth Sylvester, born January 23, 1644, daughter of Richard and Naomi (Torrey) Sylvester of Scituate. The record of the publishment and of the marriage is at Scituate: "These are to Certyfy all those to Whom It may Conscirne that John Lowwell and Elizabeth Silvester hath Been Lawfully Published accordinge to law three Lecture Dayes.

William Courssen.

Witness, Henry Bridgman.

John Lowwell abovesayed was Marryed to Elizabeth Silvester January the 24th 1658 pr Mr. Hatherly. In Scittuate."

William Courser and Henry Bridgman were residents of Boston, where the intention of marriage was published three times.

John Lowell and his wife, Elizabeth, lived in Boston until 1765, when they removed to Rehoboth. In 1669, he received grants of land in Rehoboth, where he lived until about 1680, when he removed to Lynn. After his removal from Rehoboth he was taxed a non-resident proprietor in that town about twenty years. He came from Lynn to Dunstable in 1682 or 1683. He and his sons, John and Joseph, were among the early settlers of the town and all were prominent in the affairs of the settlement. He was a selectman of Dunstable, 1689. If the records were complete it is reasonable to assume that he would have credit for other elections to office. During the troublous times of King William's War, his son, Joseph, and his three married daughters removed from Dunstable and in 1700, John, the father, and his wife, Elizabeth, were living in Sudbury. The date and place of his death have not been discovered. In 1700 then of Sudbury, he sold to William Woodcock of Rehoboth four tracts of land in Scituate and Attleborough. Until 1694, Attleborough was a part of Rehoboth. The deed is dated at Sudbury, June 20, 1700, and is recorded in the Registry of Deeds at Taunton. His wife, Elizabeth, joined in the conveyance. The original name of this family was Lowell. A person is not responsible for the form in which his name is written by the clerks of churches and towns. In the record of his publishment and marriage, the name is Lowwell. The birth of two children of John and Elizabeth Lowell is recorded in Boston. Six children were baptized at the Second Church of Scituate, now Norwood. The name of the father is written John Lowel four times, and John Lowell two times. In records of Rehoboth appear John Lowell and John Lovell, while the Lynn record presents the form of John Lovill. His name in the deed of 1700 and his signature are written John Lovwell, and here is found the easy inflection from Lowwell to Lovewell. His children, and very uniformly his descendants in Dunstable and elsewhere, have written the name Lovewell. His wife, Elizabeth Sylvester, was a daughter of Richard and Naomi (Torrey) Sylvester of Scituate. Four of their six children were born in Boston and two in Rehoboth.

2. i. JOHN, born in Boston, April 7, 1660; baptized in Scituate, June 17, 1660.
3. ii. JOSEPH, baptized, Scituate, May 25, 1662. There is no record of his birth. He was born in 1661.
   iii. PATIENCE, born in Boston, October 7, 1662; baptized in Scituate, June 7, 1663. The Vital Records of Scituate, recently published, give the date of this baptism, June 7, 1662, but the original church records say June 7, 1663. She married in Lynn, March 28, 1682, Samuel Beale. See Beale Register.
   iv. ELIZABETH, born in Boston, 1664; baptized in Scituate, August 21, 1664. She married William Beale, see.
   v. PHEBE, born in Rehoboth, December 25, 1666; baptized in Scituate, August 11, 1667; married in Chelmsford, July 24, 1685, Andrew Cooke, see.
   vi. ZACCHEUS, born in Rehoboth, December 24, 1668; died at Lynn, September 28, 1681.

2. JOHN LOVEWELL, son of John and Elizabeth (Sylvester) Lovewell, was born April 7, 1660. In childhood and

youth he lived in Rehoboth and Lynn. With the consent of his father, Joseph Sylvester, an uncle, was appointed his guardian, October 29, 1670. Probably it was
a limited guardianship relating to an inheritance from
his grandfather, Richard Sylvester, who died in 1663.
For a similar purpose and on the same day, John Lovewell, his father, was appointed guardian of Esther
Sylvester, a younger sister of his wife.

The nuncupative will of Richard Craze, who died in
Boston, was attested by Thomas Wiborne and Jabez
Heaton, April 28, 1670. They testified that the deceased
willed "ten pounds to the eldest son of John Lovell,
a tanner of Rehoboth." See New England Historic
Genealogical Register, Vol. 48, page 460.

He was one of the earliest permanent settlers of
Dunstable, coming hither with his father and brother,
1683. He was a farmer. He was industrious, honest
and respected and frequently was elected to office. He
was a selectman 1693 and probably in other years of
which the record is lost. His usefulness in life was
refreshed and renewed in the good works of his sons
and grandsons, and forever the name of Lovewell will
be honored in the annals of Dunstable.

He married at Dunstable, December 7, 1686, Anna
Hassell, born October 6, 1669, a daughter of Joseph
and Anna (Perry) Hassell of Dunstable. She died
January 5, 1754. Fox misread the record and states
that the widow of Capt. John Lovewell died January 5,
1754. The record is: "Hannah Lovewell, wife of John
Lovewell, senior, deceased ye 5 of January 1754; buried
7th." Much has been written of the extreme age of
John Lovewell and of his service in the army of Cromwell. The record is firmer and more consistent than the
traditions. His age and the age of his wife were
each ten years less than stated in the deposition dated
March 16, 1744, but such discrepancy is often met in
ancient affidavits. See Register 55, page 186. John
Lovewell very probably died in 1755, aged 95. Four
children of John and Anna (Hassell) Lovewell were
born in Dunstable.

4. i. JOHN, born October 14, 1691.
   ii. HANNAH, married Lieut. Josiah Farwell, born August 27,
       1698, son of Henry and Susannah (Richardson) Farwell.
       He was a comrade in arms with his brother-in-law, Capt.
       John Lovewell, and his lieutenant in three expeditions.
       He died on the field of battle May 8, 1725. Their only

child, *Hannah*, born January 27, 1723, married John Chamberlain of Merrimack.

5. iii. ZACCHEUS, born July 22, 1701.
6. iv. JONATHAN, born May 14, 1713.

3. JOSEPH LOVEWELL, son of John and Elizabeth (Sylvester) Lovewell, was born in Boston, 1661. He came to Dunstable with the family in 1683, and resided here about eleven years. About 1693, he removed to the part of Watertown now Weston. He was a member of the church of Watertown and when a church was organized in Weston he became a member of that church. I have not found a record of his first marriage. Mary, his wife, died in Weston, December 1, 1729. He married, second, May 5, 1730, Hannah (Johnson) Pierce, daughter of John Johnson of Cambridge and widow of Francis Pierce of Weston. He died in Weston, October 9, 1732. His widow, Hannah, died in Hopkinton in 1760. Two children of Joseph and Mary Lovewell.

7. i. JOSEPH, born in Dunstable, May 3, 1691.
   ii. MARY, born 1695. She was reared in the family of her uncle, Andrew Cooke, and was known as Mary Cooke. She married Samuel Morse, born June 4, 1687, son of Samuel and Deborah Morse. In Cambridge, Probate Records, old series, No. 10,188, is an agreement dated November 6, 1732, between Hannah, widow of Joseph Lovewell, deceased, and her two step-children, Joseph Lovewell and Mary Morse, wife of Samuel Morse. They lived in Needham, where their nine children were born and where she died November 20, 1787, aged 92. He died April 5, 1736.

4. CAPT. JOHN LOVEWELL, son of John and Anna (Hassell) Lovewell, was born in Dunstable, October 14, 1691. The danger of an exposed frontier is the efficient school of the soldier. In his childhood and youth, John Lovewell was familiar with the musket, with garrisons and with measures of defence. In his memory was the unfading story that in a single month his grandfather and grandmother, Joseph and Anna (Perry) Hassell, his uncle, Benjamin Hassell, Christopher Temple, and Obadiah Perry, who had married aunts of his mother, were slain by the merciless foe of the settlement. He recalled that in 1706. five soldiers and six of his neighbors were slain within the town of Dunstable. He was twelve years of age and too young for service when Capt. William Tyng, commanding the first company of snow shoe men, returned to Dunstable with

trophies of victory. He saw the scalps of Indians
borne in triumph and in the inspiration of his surround-
ings he constantly advanced to the higher grades in the
school of the soldier.

Succeeding these events there were a few years of
peace with the Indians. The war was renewed in 1723
and again the hardy men of the frontiers assumed an
attitude of defence. In 1724, four were captured and
eight were killed by the Indians in this town. John
Lovewell immediately proposed to raise a company and
to march into the haunts of the enemy. He was commissioned a captain and at the same time Josiah Farwell was commissioned a lieutenant and Jonathan
Robbins, ensign. In the last week of November, 1724,
with thirty men, including officers, Capt. Lovewell set
out on a tedious march to the region of Lake Winne-
pesaukee, and December 10, the company killed one
Indian and captured two, one of the captives being
a boy. The second expedition marched from Dunstable
January 29, 1725, including officers there were eighty-
eight men in the company. After a few days thirty
men were sent home on account of a scarcity of provisions. When near the lake, February 21, 1725, the
company killed ten Indians and then set out for Boston
to obtain the bounty offered for Indian scalps. They
were at Dover February 23, and arrived in Boston
March 9, 1725. The Journal of Capt. Lovewell of this
march is found in New England Historic Genealogical
Register, Vol. 7, page 62. The third company under the
same officers marched from Dunstable, April 15, 1725.
Including officers there were forty-seven men. Three
were honorably excused during the outward march,
ten were left at a fort erected in Ossipee and thirty-
four were on duty under Capt. Lovewell in the morning of the memorable battle, May 8, 1725. Of these,
Capt. Lovewell and eleven others were killed and buried
on the field of battle; three were mortally wounded
and died near the scene of conflict; nine were more or
less seriously wounded; nine escaped without wounds
and one retired from the field and fled to the fort in the
early progress of the battle. For a more extended account of the three expeditions commanded by Capt.
Lovewell, see Historical Sermon by Rev. Thomas
Symmes of Bradford; "The Expeditions of Capt. John
Lovewell" by Frederick Kidder and sketches in historical publications. The names of all the men of the

third expedition with condensed sketches are found in in the Register, Vol. 63, page 288. It is remarkable that a record of the marriage of Capt. John Lovewell has not been discovered, or that tradition does not make known the full name of his wife. Her Christian name was Hannah. She was the executrix of his estate and a few years later married Benjamin Smith of Merrimack, in whose family her children were reared. See Smith Register. Three children of Capt. John and Hannah Lovewell.

8. i. JOHN, born June 30, 1718.
   ii. HANNAH, born July 24, 1721; married May 31, 1739, Capt. Joseph Baker, born in Roxbury, Mass., January 25, 1714, son of Thomas and Sarah (Pike) Baker. The township of Suncook, now Pembroke, was granted to the forty-seven men of Capt. Lovewell's third expedition and to make the number sixty, thirteen men of the second expedition were made grantees. Mrs. Baker inherited one-third of the right granted to the heirs of Capt. John Lovewell. They settled in Pembroke, where their eleven children were born. Their descendants are numerous and among those well-known to the present generation are Mary Baker Eddy, Hon. Henry M. Baker of Bow, N. H., and others.
9. iii. NEHEMIAH, born January 9, 1725-6, posthumous.

5. COL. ZACCHEUS LOVEWELL, son of John and Anna (Hassell) Lovewell, was born in Dunstable July 22, 1701. Imbued with a military spirit, which distinguishes the family, he was early engaged in the Indian Wars and was promoted to the rank of major. In 1759, he was commissioned a colonel and given the command of a regiment of one thousand men for the reduction of Canada. Of his regiment John Goffe was lieutenant colonel but only a fragment of the rolls are preserved. In 1760, the militia of the province was reorganized and Zaccheus Lovewell was commissioned colonel of the fifth regiment and held the position until 1767, when he was succeeded by Edward Goldstone Lutwyche. He lived a few years before 1740 in Nottingham West, now Hudson, and was a moderator and selectman of that town. Later he was a prominent and useful citizen of Dunstable, where he was frequently elected to office. In reward for his service in the Indian wars he was one of the six grantees of 2190 acres adjoining Pembroke. He died at Dunstable, April 12, 1772. He married Esther Hassell, born in Dunstable, July 30, 1709, a daughter of Joseph Hassell, Jr. Nine children.

       i. ZACCHEUS, born February 19, 1726-7; died young.
      ii. ESTHER, born November 20, 1728.
     iii. LUCY, born January 12, 1730-1; married Joseph Blanchard, see.
     iv. MOLLY, born May 26, 1732; married Capt. Benjamin French, son of Joseph French, see.
      v. ZACCHEUS, born December 15, 1735.
10. vi. NOAH, born April 1, 1742.
     vii. SARAH, born October 25, 1744.
    viii. HANNAH, born February 17, 1747; married May 31, 1761, Joseph Hale. They lived in Dunstable, where eight children were born. He was a son of Thomas Hale, being of a branch of the Heald family who wrote the name Hale.
     ix. BRIDGET, born July 10, 1749; married Augustus Blanchard, a son of Col. Joseph Blanchard, see.

6. JONATHAN LOVEWELL, son of John and Anna (Hassell) Lovewell, was born in Dunstable, May 14, 1713. He lived in an historic era. In childhood and youth he was inured to the dangers of the frontier and the extreme cruelties of Indian warfare. His active life covered the golden age of the province under the Wentworths, the Revolution, and the early years of the independent state of New Hampshire. He was active and prominent in town affairs and frequently elected to office. He was a representative in the provincial house of representatives during the session which convened September 19, 1752, and dissolved September 18, 1755. In this service his record is conspicuous. At the session convened November 14, 1758, Mr. Lovewell appeared for Dunstable and Dr. John Hale for Dunstable and Hollis, both being elected the same day and by two sections of the same meeting. The house of representatives declared the elections void and refused to admit either of the gentlemen. Through the temper of Gov. Wentworth, the session was abruptly dissolved, February 4, 1762, and a new election of representatives was held throughout the province. The house convened March 10, 1762, and Dr. John Hale of Hollis, who had been elected for Dunstable and Hollis, was admitted.

    Dunstable was incorporated by New Hampshire, April 1, 1746. There was a division of sentiment concerning the settlement of Rev. Samuel Bird. The first town meeting was rent in twain. Zaccheus Lovewell was the moderator of one meeting and Jonathan Lovewell was the clerk of the other. An appeal was pre-

sented to the general court. Those opposed to Mr. Bird
were represented by Col. Joseph Blanchard and the
friends of Mr. Bird were represented by Jonathan Lovewell.
It was a vigorous contest occupying two days.
The general court declared both meetings illegal.
He was a collector of excise several years beginning
1753. For the expedition to Crown Point, 1755, the
general court appointed Jonathan Lovewell a commissary
of the regiment commanded by Col. Joseph
Blanchard. In 1768, some difficulty arose in the collection
of taxes of Amherst, and an appeal was made to
the general court for relief. The subject was referred
to Jonathan Lovewell, Edward Goldstone Lutwyche
and Samuel Patten with instructions to collect evidence
and report the facts to the general court. In the Revolution
he was a delegate from Dunstable in the first,
second, fourth and fifth provincial congresses. In the
third congress Dunstable was represented by Joseph
Ayers. The fifth congress adopted a temporary constitution
and by resolution became the first house of
representatives of the state of New Hampshire. He
was a member of the House of Representatives during
the two succeeding years and was twice elected one of
the State Committee of Safety. For many years he was
a justice of the peace and January 26, 1776, he was appointed
chief justice of the Court of Common Pleas for
the County of Hillsborough. At the reorganization of
the courts under the permanent constitution, Judge
Lovewell was succeeded in 1784 by Judge Timothy
Farrar.

Jonathan Lovewell married in Newbury, Mass.,
October 16, 1734, Bridget Honey, daughter of Peter
Honey, see. It is probable that she died within a few
years after marriage. He died in 1792, and sleeps in
an unmarked grave, but his name lives and his memory
abides in the annals of Dunstable and of New Hampshire.
No children.

7. JOSEPH LOVEWELL, son of Joseph and Mary Lovewell,
was born in Dunstable, May 3, 1691. In his early
childhood, the family removed to Weston, where he
resided through his subsequent life. He married December
22, 1714, Deborah Morse, born January 10, 1690,
a daughter of Samuel and Deborah Morse. He died
January 23, 1763. His wife, Deborah, died January 19,
1764. Ten children.

i. JOSEPH, born 1715; died December 31, 1726.
　　　ii. DEBORAH, born June 14, 1719; died in September, 1719.
　　　iii. DEBORAH, born October 31, 1720; died July 3, 1725.
　　　iv. ISAAC, born May 4, 1723; died November 13, 1735.
　　　v. DEBORAH, born October 4, 1725; married 1750, Samuel Ware. They lived in Needham, where five children were born.
　　　vi. MARY, born March 15, 1727.
11.　vii. JOSEPH, born October 27, 1729.
　　　viii. ELIZABETH, born February 4, 1731-2; died November 28, 1748.
　　　ix. HANNAH, born 1734; died 1734.
　　　x. PATIENCE, twin, born 1734; died 1734.

8. JOHN LOVEWELL, son of Capt. John and Hannah Lovewell, was born in Dunstable, June 30, 1718. He was an active and respected citizen of Dunstable where he died July 2, 1762. He was commissioned a lieutenant in 1745. He married at Hampton Falls, N. H., November 2, 1739, Rachel Lund, daughter of William Lund of Dunstable, see. Seven children, born in Dunstable.

　　　i. RACHEL, born May 18, 1740.
　　　ii. ANNA, born February 29, 1742-3; died in August, 1758.
　　　iii. JOHN, born November 16, 1744. He was a soldier in the Revolution, serving in Capt. Walker's company at Bunker Hill and siege of Boston, 1775; in Capt. Read's company of Col. Baldwin's regiment, 1776; in Lieut. Brown's company at Saratoga, 1777; and in Capt. Frye Bailey's company, Vermont service, in later years. He removed to Corinth, Vermont, probably in 1778, where he died April 18, 1815. He married Vodica Lovewell, daughter of Capt. Nehemiah Lovewell, see. Five children. *Sophia*, who married Jacob Mills; *Hannah; Louisa; John*, who died unmarried; *Nehemiah*, born 1803, married Martha Mills. Two of the sons of Nehemiah and Martha (Mills) Lovewell, John, and Joseph Taplin Lovewell, are graduates of Yale.
　　　iv. JONATHAN, born August 20, 1747; married November 14, 1783, Caty Honey, daughter of John and Elizabeth Honey, see. He died March 15, 1788; his widow married, second, February 3, 1791, Theodore French, see.
　　　v. MARY, born March 10, 1749.
　　　vi. JAMES, born October 15, 1752; died November 27, 1753.
　　　vii. ZACCHEUS, born May 22, 1756; died October 8, 1758.

9. COL. NEHEMIAH LOVEWELL, son of Capt. John and Hannah Lovewell, was born at Dunstable, January 9, 1726,

posthumous. He was reared at Merrimack in the family of his step-father, Benjamin Smith. He married at Dunstable, November 24, 1748, Rachel Farwell, a daughter of Jonathan and Susannah (Blanchard) Farwell. After his marriage he lived in Dunstable over twenty years, occupying a prominent position in town affairs. In the French and Indian War he served in three campaigns. He was a lieutenant of Col. Blanchard's regiment, 1755, a captain of Col. Hart's regiment, 1758 and a captain of Col. Goffe's regiment, 1760. In 1770, he removed from Dunstable to Newbury, Vt., and was in the service almost continuously during the Revolution. He was a captain of Col. Bedel's regiment 1777 and 1778, and also of Major Wait's battalion of rangers and in this service he was captured but soon released. In the border warfare he commanded companies and military posts almost continuously from 1779 to 1782. After the war he was a colonel of the militia. Soon after the Revolution he removed to Corinth, Vermont, where he died March 23, 1801. He was an honest, industrious, efficient man.

Of Col. Nehemiah and Rachel (Farwell) Lovewell there were thirteen children born in Dunstable, the youngest being an infant when the family removed to Vermont.

i. CATHERINE, born June 17, 1749; married September 29, 1769, Major John Taplin, born 1748, son of Col. John and Hepsibah (Brigham) Taplin. He was a soldier in the French and Indian War and in the Revolution. He removed from Newbury to Corinth, Vt., and was sheriff of the county. Subsequently he lived in Berlin and in Montpelier. Through the active years of his life he was conspicuous in town and state affairs. His wife, Catherine, died July 16, 1794. He married, second, Lydia Gove, who died February 11, 1849. He died 1835. Twelve children.

ii. SUSANNAH, born July 22, 1750; died October 26, 1758.

iii. HANNAH, born July 22, 1750, twin; died October 31, 1758.

iv. NEHEMIAH, born July 1, 1752. Soldier in the Revolution. He was at Bunker Hill and later a captain of Col. Herrick's and Col. Fletcher's regiments. He married August 8, 1781, Betsey Haseltine, born, Newbury, Vt., May 4, 1763, daughter of John and Sarah (Bedel) Haseltine. He was a farmer and innholder in Newbury, Vt., where he died, July 14, 1801. She died November 18, 1850.

v. BETSEY, born June 25, 1754; married Mansfield Taplin, a brother of Major John Taplin. Lived at Corinth.

vi. HENRY, born January 9, 1757. He served in Capt. Walker's company at Bunker Hill and siege of Boston, 1775, in Col. Bedel's regiment, 1778, and in the frontier service of Vermont. He died in Orleans County, New York, 1812.

vii. ZACCHEUS, born November 8, 1758. In the Revolution he served in his father's company of Col. Bedel's regiment and in several companies of Vermont organizations commanded by Capt. Thomas Johnson, Capt. Simeon Stevens, Capt. Nehemiah Lovewell, Capt. John G. Bailey, and was a sergeant at Fort Wait in Corinth. He married Hepsibah Taplin, who was the mother of seven children: *Zaccheus, Betsey, Hepsibah, Joseph Bliss, Moodey Bedel, William* and *Jonathan*. Hepsibah, wife of Zaccheus, died about 1800. He married, second, Irene Lyman Loveland, by whom he had three children; Nehemiah, Samuel and Lyman. Of these, Nehemiah, born February 1, 1803, married July 20, 1826, Sarah C. Hubbard, married, second, August 19, 1845, Phebe (Cole) Hill. He was a surveyor, living several years in Orleans County, New York, and beginning 1855, at Coldwater, Michigan. He died in Chicago, Illinois, January 3, 1890. His youngest son, Charles Hubert Lovewell, M. D., born October 9, 1848, University of Michigan, M. D., 1871, is a skillful physician of Chicago.

viii. JONATHAN, born November 7, 1760; married May 28, 1801, Sophia Taplin. He was a farmer of Corinth, where he died January 1, 1817. Four children.

ix. ROBERT, born October 1, 1762; married January 2, 1787, Polly Taplin, a sister of Major John, Mansfield, Sophia and Hepsibah, who married sisters and brothers of Robert. He was in Capt. Farnsworth's company at battle of Plattsburg. He lived at St. Albans, Vermont. He died September 4, 1838. His wife died November 10, 1869. Nine children.

x. VODICA, born April 18, 1764. In record of birth at Dunstable, the name is written Noadica. She married her cousin, John Lovewell, son of John and grandson of Capt. John, see.

xi. JOHN, born March 18, 1766; married Sally (Drew) Bailey.

xii. JOSEPH, born January 6, 1768.

xiii. RACHEL, born June 8, 1770; married Samuel Hillard.

10. GEN. NOAH LOVEWELL, son of Col. Zaccheus and Esther (Hassell) Lovewell, was born in Dunstable, April 1, 1742. He married December 17, 1767, Mary Farwell, born January 10, 1745, daughter of Oliver and Abigail (Hubbard) Farwell. He was one of the most prominent and useful men who have lived in Dunstable. At the beginning of the Revolution he was a captain of the Dunstable company and in the reorganization of the fifth regiment he was commissioned lieutenant colonel

of Col. Moses Nichols' regiment. In raising men and
as one of the paymasters of the state he proved an efficient officer and in mean time he was one of the commissioners for Hillsborough county, having charge and
conducting the sale of the confiscated estates of the
loyalists. He was appointed colonel of the regiment,
succeeding Col. Nichols, March 30, 1781, and in the
reorganization of the militia under the constitution, he
was commissioned colonel of the fifth regiment, December 21, 1784, and promoted to brigadier general November 7, 1788. He was the first postmaster of Dunstable,
a selectman many years and a delegate to the fourth
provincial congress and a representative from December, 1778, to December, 1779. Under the state constitution of 1784, he was a representative several years
and maintained a foremost position among able colleagues. He died May 29, 1820. His widow, Mary,
died November 24, 1835.

  i. MOLLY, born August 24, 1768; married November 24, 1790,
     Giles Shurtleff, born in Middleton, Mass. January
     19, 1768, son of Jonathan and Elizabeth (Leach) Shurtleff.
     They lived in Dunstable several years when they removed
     to Croydon, N. H., where he died, 1820. They had six
     children.

 ii. ABIGAIL, born June 19, 1770; married February 27, 1786, Israel
     Whitney Cummings, born in Hudson, N. H., August 23,
     1762, son of Eleazer and Hannah (Whitney) Cummings. Lived in Woodstock and Thetford, Vt. He died
     February 19, 1836. She died March 13, 1845. Three
     children.

iii. ZACCHEUS, born June 10, 1772.

 iv. ESTHER, born June 9, 1774; died October 17, 1777.

  v. NOAH, born November 11, 1776; died May 6, 1777.

 vi. JOHN, born February 10, 1778.

vii. ESTHER, born May 16, 1780; married Luther Taylor, see.

viii. NOAH, born September 2, 1782.

 ix. MOODY DUSTIN, born March 1, 1785.

  x. BETSEY, born March 2, 1788; married Hon. Jesse Bowers,
     November 12, 1785, son of William and Hannah(Kidder)
     Bowers of Chelmsford. They lived in Dunstable. He was
     a representative and state senator and prominent in financial affairs. Of their six children, a daughter, Mary
     Augusta, married Gen. John Bedel of Bath.

11. JOSEPH LOVEWELL, son of Joseph and Deborah (Morse)
Lovewell, born in Weston, October 27, 1729. He was

a soldier in the French and Indian War and was captured by the enemy. After a fortunate escape from captivity, he suffered extreme hardship while returning to his home. He married November 2, 1761, Hannah Warren, born November 1, 1741, daughter of Daniel and Deborah (Phillips) Warren of Concord, Massachusetts. He lived in Weston. He is the ancestor of all the descendants in male lines of Joseph Lovewell of Dunstable and Weston. Hannah, his wife, died October 8, 1782. He married, second, March 10, 1794, Ruth (Child) Walker, widow of John Walker. He died 1801; Ruth, his widow, died 1809. Ten children.

i. ISAAC, born July 23, 1762; married April 9, 1788, Lucy Harrington, born 1752, daughter of Adino and Esther (Hastings) Harrington. Removed to Livermore, Me. She died March 6, 1807. He married, second, Widow Lucy Merrill. He died November 10, 1835. She died July 23, 1856. Four children.

ii. JOSEPH, born October 2, 1763; married at Templeton, April 10, 1796, Sarah Wilkinson, born, Needham, May 9, 1768, daughter of Ebenezer and Mary (Gay) Wilkinson. He removed to Hubbardston, Massachusetts. His descendants are numerous. He died November 21, 1814. She died August 29, 1847. Seven children.

iii. NATHAN, born April 21, 1765. He lived in Lancaster, N. H., and in Lunenburg, Vt. He married December 27, 1792, Charlotte Stockwell, born Lancaster, October 24, 1770, daughter of Emmons and Ruth (Page) Stockwell. He died November 16, 1819; she died February 26, 1816. Eleven children.

iv. JONATHAN, born April 6, 1768; married April 6, 1806, Elizabeth Goldthwait. He lived in Weston, where two sons, Daniel and George, were born. He died 1813.

v. DANIEL, born July 31, 1770; married in Brookline, Mass., November 20, 1790, Nancy Jackson, born 1770, daughter of Thaddeus and Lydia (Woodward) Jackson. Removed to Livermore, Maine, where he died 1803. She married, second, Samuel Webster and died in Brookline, March 18, 1861. Three children, *Amasa* and *Luther*, twins, born February 11, 1796; *Hannah J.*, born 1805, unmarried, died December 25, 1885.

vi. SAMUEL, born 1772; baptized April 26, 1772. He lived in Weston, where he died August 3, 1851. He married August 4, 1796, Abigail Bartlett, born Newton, Mass., June 26, 1766, daughter of Ebenezer and Anna (Ball) Bartlett. She died, the mother of three children, May 13, 1811. He married, second, February 11, 1812, Chloe Rice, born November 25, 1776, daughter of Isaac and Sarah (Lamb) Rice of East Sudbury, Mass. She died, leaving one son, May 15, 1825. He married, third, January 9, 1826, Asenath Goodnow, born Framingham, Mass., January 3, 1794, daughter of Ephraim and Nelly (Rice) Goodnow. She was the mother

Thirty Dunstable Families. 47

of two children. She died February 26, 1836. He married, fourth, March 27, 1838, Widow Jane Whitney. She died 1839. Prof. Samuel Harrison Lovewell, a cultured musician, and now president and director of the Conservatory of Music, Quincy, Illinois, has made an exhaustive study of the Joseph Lovewell family. He is a son of Charles Baker and Martha Jane (Morse) Lovewell, and a grandson of Samuel and Asenath (Goodnow) Lovewell.

vii. ELIZABETH, born March 2, 1774; married Peter Godding, born, Watertown, October 28, 1763, son of Jonathan Coolidge and Hannah (Learned) Godding. They lived in Livermore, Me. Twelve children.

viii. HANNAH, born 1777; baptized June 1, 1777; married Spencer Godding, born, Watertown, 1769, a brother of Peter Godding, who married her sister, Elizabeth. He died in Livermore, 1856. She died 1847. Nine children.

ix. RHODA, born 1779, removed to Philadelphia, Pa., there married John Baker, a shipwright who died 1809. She married, second, 1817, Joseph Sabins, a sea captain. She died February 2, 1871.

x. DELIVERANCE, born October 7, 1782; married William Cooper.

12. ICHABOD LOVEWELL, not placed but a son of one of the Dunstable families of Lovewell, served continuously in the army of the Revolution from May, 1775 until his death. He served in Capt. William Walker's company at Bunker Hill and siege of Boston, 1775, in one of the Continental regiments at Ticonderoga and in New Jersey, 1776, and in Col. Cilley's regiment from April 1, 1777, until his death in July, 1777.

LUND. On the roll of the company of Capt. Nathaniel Davenport, in King Philip's War, 1676, appears the name of Nicholas Lunn of Reading, and later in the same year he was a soldier stationed at Chelmsford. From the fact that he or his legal representatives did not apply for a right in any of the Narragansett townships, it is probable that he died without issue. There is no evidence that he was related to the Dunstable family of the same name.

Thomas Lund was a trader of Boston. July 18, 1650, he applied to and secured from William Aspinwall, the Recorder of the Suffolk County Court and a Notary Public, a protest against William Greene, master of the ship *Swallow*, from London, for the reason that the ship did not sail on the tenth day of March, 1649, according to promise, but did sail March 29, and that said master did not take into said ship all the goods of the said Lunn. The same notary issues a certificate, dated March 18, 1650, that the ship *Speedwell*, of London, had delivered to Thomas Lunne, merchant of Boston, one butt, contents 1600 & quarter wht. Currans.

March 16, 1672, Thomas Lunn was a witness to a deed of Samuel Bennett to Benjamin Muzzey of Rumney Marsh, conveying land in Boston. He died before February 5, 1677, when administration on the estate of Thomas Lun, late of Boston, seaman, was granted to Benjamin Muzzey, Senior, of Rumney Marsh, in the right of Thomas the only child of said deceased.

1. THOMAS LUND, the only child of Thomas, came to Dunstable about 1680, and was one of the proprietors of the township. During the troublous times of King William's War, many of the families of Dunstable removed to the older towns. In a petition to the General Court preferred by Major Thomas Henchman, commander of the garrisons in this vicinity, he says: All the inhabitants of Dunstable, excepting two families, desire to draw off, viz.: John Solendine and Thomas Lunn, whose garrisons are near to each other. For many years during seasons of alarm his house was one of the fortified garrisons of the settlement.

   He was a selectman and a useful citizen. He and his sons, Thomas and William, owned valuable and extensive tracts of land and the record of many deeds are at Cambridge and after 1741, at Concord, N. H. He was living in 1721, but there is no record of his death or of Eleanor, his wife. Four children.

2.   i. THOMAS, born September 9, 1682.
     ii. ELIZABETH, born September 29, 1684; married Henry Spalding, born November 2, 1680, son of Andrew and Hannah (Jefts) Spalding. They lived in Chelmsford.
3.   iii. WILLIAM, born January 25, 1686-7.
     iv. MARGARET, married in Concord, January 16, 1711-2, Lieut. Jonathan Robbins, see. Married, second, William Shattuck of Groton.

2. THOMAS LUND, son of Thomas and Eleanor Lund, was born in Dunstable, September 9, 1682. He married in Concord, Mass., January 16, 1711-2, Elizabeth Taylor, born August 7, 1690, daughter of Abraham and Mary (Whitaker) Taylor and a sister of Abraham Taylor of Dunstable. In 1723, he was a soldier in Capt. Jabez Fairbank's company, which was engaged in scouting for the protection of Dunstable, Groton, Lunenburg and Lancaster. He was one of the snow shoe men in

Thirty Dunstable Families. 49

Capt. Tyng's company, 1703-4, and was one of the eight men slain by the Indians near Thornton's ferry, September 5, 1724.

Administration on the estate of "Thomas Lund, killed by the Indian enemy," was granted to his widow, Elizabeth, October 22, 1724. David Taylor of Concord, her brother, was surety on her bond. The inventory was £408-10.

The widow, Elizabeth, married, second, Isaac Cummings and lived in Dunstable.

October 30, 1744, Thomas Lund, Jonathan Lund, Phineas Lund, all of Dunstable, and Edward Spalding and wife, Elizabeth of Nottingham, all children of Thomas Lund of Dunstable, deceased, sell to our brother, Ephraim Lund of Dunstable, their right in the dower of our mother, Elizabeth Cummings, formerly widow of Thomas Lund. Five children of Thomas and Elizabeth (Taylor) Lund.

4.   i.   THOMAS, born October 31, 1712.
     ii.   ELIZABETH, born May 14, 1715; married Edward Spalding, born in Chelmsford, March 8, 1707-8, son of Ebenezer Spalding. They lived in Hudson, where five children were born.
5.   iii.   JONATHAN, born October 12, 1717.
6.   iv.   EPHRAIM, born August 3, 1720.
7.   v.   PHINEAS, born April 3, 1723.

3. WILLIAM LUND, son of Thomas and Eleanor Lund, was born in Dunstable, January 25, 1686-7. In 1724 "while in the service of his country" he was captured by the Indians and conducted to Canada. In his petition to the General Court he alleges that "he suffered great hardships and was obliged to pay a great price for his ransom." He returned to his home before the expiration of many months and enlisted into the company of Capt. Eleazer Tyng, and served from June 10 to November 10, 1725. Early in the service of this company they marched to the field of Capt. Lovewell's fight and there buried twelve men who fell in that memorable engagement.

In consideration of his misfortune and suffering while in captivity the General Court of Massachusetts, in 1734, granted to William Lund four hundred acres of land which was surveyed in 1737. The grant was located in Goffstown. In 1739, in consideration of £400, he sold

Thirty Dunstable Families.

the grant to Francis Borland of Boston. He owned many parcels of land in Dunstable, Hudson and Merrimack. He married at Groton, December 20, 1716, Rachel Holden, daughter of Stephen and Hannah (Lawrence) Holden of Groton, and granddaughter of Richard and Martha (Fosdick) Holden of Cambridge. He died about 1758. His will was proved February 28, 1759. Five children.

8.   i. WILLIAM, born July 18, 1717.
    ii. RACHEL, born August 28, 1719; married John Lovewell, son of Capt. John Lovewell, see.
9.   iii. CHARITY, born February 16, 1730-1.
    iv. MARY, born November 28, 1733; married James Underwood.
    v. LUCY, born May 26, 1736; died young.

4. DEA. THOMAS LUND, son of Thomas and Elizabeth (Taylor) Lund, was born in Dunstable, October 31, 1712. He was a deacon, a town officer and a prominent citizen of Dunstable. He owned many parcels of land and his name as grantor or grantee frequently appears in the records. His first wife was Mary. A record of his marriage has not been discovered. She died January 14, 1748. He married, second, Sarah, who died April 16, 1801. He died February 24, 1790.

    i. JESSE, born March 10, 1737; died September 8, 1738.
10. ii. THOMAS, born March 12, 1740.
11. iii. JOEL, born November 27, 1752.
    iv. SARAH, born February 24, 1755; married December 9, 1779, James Jewell.
    v. PHEBE, born April 15, 1757; married December 18, 1781, Thomas Roby.
    vi. NOAH, born March 31, 1759; married December 6, 1786, Betty Hale.
    vii. MARY born November 7, 1760; married January 8, 1784, Nehemiah Wright, born October 12, 1756, son of John and Mary (Kendall) Wright. Removed to Nelson.
    viii. DANIEL, born October 31, 1762; married January 25, 1791, Hepsibah Hunt, born September 5, 1766, daughter of William and Mary (Hardy) Hunt of Dunstable.
    ix. BETTY, born October 15, 1766.
    x. DOLLY, born July 8, 1768.
    xi. LYDIA, born July 8, 1768, twin.
    xii. HANNAH, born October 5, 1769.

Thirty Dunstable Families. 51

5. CAPT. JONATHAN LUND, son of Thomas and Elizabeth Taylor) Lund, was born in Dunstable, October 12, 1717. He was a leading citizen of the town, a captain in the militia and a selectman. He married at Dunstable, April 9, 1741, Jean Varnum, born at Dracut, April 13, 1713, daughter of Thomas and Joanna (Jewett) Varnum. She died September 14, 1764. He married, second, October 22, 1765, Olive Sargent, a daughter of Dr. Nathaniel and Ruth (Jackson) Sargent of New Castle and Portsmouth. He died November 29, 1801. Six children of the first and five of the second wife.

 i. OLIVE, born March 15, 1742.

 ii. JOANNA, born September 16, 1743; married October 6, 1763. Dea. Benjamin Smith. He died in Dunstable, March 29, 1821. Joanna, his wife, died August 21, 1814.

 iii. JONATHAN, born July 24, 1747. He married Priscilla Cummings, born July 7, 1747, daughter of Ephraim and Elizabeth (Butler) Cummings. In company with Jonathan Danforth, he built a saw mill on Witch brook in 1766, then in Monson and now in Hollis, near the line of Amherst. He was a blacksmith, and his farm in Milford has been the poor farm of Milford. He died June 11, 1828. Priscilla, his wife, died January 22, 1824. See History of Milford, N. H., for a record of ten children.

 iv. MARY, born August 24, 1749; died November 17, 1758.

 v. OLIVER, born July 29, 1752; died March 18, 1776.

 vi. MEHITABLE, born June 19, 1755; died November 28, 1758.

 vii. JOSEPH, born December 24, 1767. He lived in Dunstable, where he died August 21, 1835. His widow, Betsey, died December 3, 1863. Their son, Joseph S. Lund, died in Concord, N. H. December 27, 1882.

 viii. NATHANIEL.

 ix. OLIVE, married 1800, Aaron Whitney, born 1772, son of Levi Whitney of Townsend. He lived in Amherst and in Calais, Maine.

 x. ELIZABETH.

 xi. JAMES TAYLOR.

6. EPHRAIM LUND, son of Thomas and Elizabeth (Taylor) Lund, was born in Dunstable, August 3, 1720; he married Rachel Pierce, born in Groton, October 21, 1723, daughter of Stephen and Rachel Pierce. He lived in Amherst and in Dunstable until 1765, when he removed to Plymouth, N. H. He was the first town clerk of Plymouth and one of the first board of selectmen and he built the first mill in Plymouth. He removed in

1770 to Warren, N. H. Later he lived in Benton, where he died about 1796. It is probable that he had a second wife, Esther, but a record is not found.

  i. RACHEL, born August 29, 1743.

12. ii. EPHRAIM, born August 25, 1745.

  iii. ELIZABETH, born October 23, 1748.

  iv. STEPHEN, born July 1, 1751. He was a soldier in Col. Bedel's regiment in 1778. He lived in Warren, a pensioner, where he died 1843.

  v. JOSEPH, born April 28, 1754. He served in Col. Bedel's regiment 1776. He was a temporary resident of Benton, but lived many years in Warren.

  vi. NOADIAH, born March 10, 1757, a soldier in the Revolution from Warren.

  vii. SUSANNAH, born September 17, 1759.

  viii. SILAS, born September 12, 1762, lived in Warren.

Stephen Pierce, the father of Mrs. Lund, died in Groton, July 6, 1761. Articles of agreement concerning the estate made September 16, 1761, and recorded in Middlesex Registry, Vol. 68, page 436, are signed by the widow, Rachel Pierce, sons Jonathan and Stephen and Ephraim Lund and his wife Rachel, Jonathan Gilson and his wife Susannah, Nathan Fiske and his wife Mary, and by two unmarried daughters, Elizabeth and Thankful Pierce.

7. PHINEAS LUND, son of Thomas, Jr., born April 3, 1723. He lived in Dunstable, Lyndeborough and Amherst. He died in Amherst, December 2, 1818, aged 95. A record of his marriage has not been discovered. Nine children were born in Dunstable.

  i. LUCY, born January 31, 1745; married March 21, 1776, Benjamin Shepard of Amherst.

  ii. RHODA, born August 30, 1748.

  iii. SAMUEL FRENCH, born July 25, 1751.

  iv. JESSE, born March 20, 1757. He was a soldier in the Revolution, and was wounded at Bunker Hill. Later he served on the quota of Harvard, Mass., 1777 to 1780. One Jesse Lund married in Bolton, Mass., July 25, 1803, Caty Parker.

  v. BRIDGET, born August 30, 1759; married February 24, 1791, Isaac Parkhurst ef Temple.

  vi. WILLARD, born February 21, 1762; married Sarah Towne daughter of Thomas and Sarah (Burton) Towne of Temple.

vii. CATHERINE, born July 22, 1764.
viii. SARAH, born February 19, 1768.
ix. RACHEL, born May 21, 1771; married about 1819, Jacob Duncklee of Amherst. His second marriage.

8. WILLIAM LUND, son of William and Rachel (Holden) Lund, was born in Dunstable, July 18, 1717. He was a farmer and a respected townsman. He married Sarah. He died March 20, 1782. Nine children.

  i. HANNAH, born June 18, 1743; married William Roby. She died in Dunstable, June 11, 1838.
  ii. WILLIAM, born May 11, 1745; died young.
  iii. SARAH, born April 4, 1747; married James Whitney; married, second, Isaac Pike.
13 iv. JOHN, born February 22, 1749.
  v. MARY, born April 17, 1752.
  vi. LEVI, born December 12, 1754; married April 8, 1784, Sarah Cutler who died May 28, 1785. He married, second, Naomi Gibson. He died December 23, 1814. His descendants are numerous.
  vii. REBECCA, born March 15, 1757; married July 30, 1782, Daniel Woods, born February 15, 1760, son of Oliver and Sarah Woods of Dunstable.
  viii. WILLIAM, born July 1, 1758. He was killed in the army of the Revolution.
  ix. AUGUSTUS, born December 17, 1764; married April 10, 1787, Joanna Smith, born in Dunstable, October 31, 1763, daughter of Dea. Benjamin and Joanna (Lund) Smith. They lived in Dunstable and in Merrimack. Ten children.

9. CHARITY LUND, son of William, born February 16, 1730-1; married Lucy. He settled in Merrimack. He was a successful farmer. There is no record of the birth of his children. His will was probated June 25, 1793, and mention therein is made of wife Lucy, sons Charity, Stephen, John, James, Cosmo, William Jarathmeel and daughters Lucy, Elizabeth, Rachel, Sarah, Hannah, and Rebecca.

  The descendants of Charity Lund are numerous, but a record with dates is not at my command. His son, Stephen, married September, 1785, Lucy Danforth, born January 6, 1766, daughter of Joseph and Mary (Richardson) Danforth. Stephen, son of Stephen and Lucy (Danforth) Lund, born in Merrimack, March 3, 1789, married in Hollis, September 12, 1810, Elizabeth Ober; married, second, in Hollis, June 2, 1813, Mary Hardy, born May 9, 1792, daughter of Nehemiah Hardy of Hollis. He lived in Merrimack. Charles Tylor Lund of Nashua is a grandson of Stephen Lund, Jr.

10. THOMAS LUND, son of Thomas, Jr., born March 12, 1740. He married Sarah Whitney. Eight children were born in Dunstable. He died February, 1821. His widow died December, 1831.
    i. BETTY, born October 15, 1766.
    ii. DOLLY, born July 8, 1768; married September 15, 1794, John Read.
    iii. HANNAH, born October 5, 1769.
    iv. JOHN, born 1772.
    v. THOMAS.
    vi. ISAAC.
    vii. OLIVER, born April 8, 1779; married March 18, 1815, Orpah Danforth, born January 2, 1789, daughter of Capt. William and Lucy (Pollard) Danforth. He died December 21, 1866; she died March 2, 1867.
    viii. SARAH.
    ix. NOAH.
    x. HULDAH.

11. JOEL LUND, son of Thomas, Jr., born November 27, 1752. He was a lieutenant in the Revolution. He married Sarah.
    i. JOEL, born October 18, 1773; married November 8, 1803, Priscilla Lund, born January 25, 1779, daughter of Jonathan, Jr., and Priscilla (Cummings) Lund of Milford. He lived in Hollis and in Nashua.
    ii. SARAH, born November 23, 1777.
    iii. JANE, born April 17, 1784.
    iv. BETSEY, born August 16, 1787.

12. EPHRAIM LUND, son of Ephraim and Rachel (Pierce) Lund, was born in Dunstable, August 25, 1745. He went to Plymouth in 1765, with his father, and in 1770 to Warren. Little's History of Warren says he died in the army during the Revolution. According to the records of the family he returned from Grafton county and settled in Hollis.

    Ephraim Lund of Hollis served in Capt. Daniel Emerson's company in 1777, and was a prosperous farmer of that town. He married in Hollis, May 12,

Thirty Dunstable Families.   55

1772, Alice Wheeler, born December 1, 1745, daughter of Peter and Hannah (Colburn) Wheeler of Bedford, Mass., and Hollis. He died in Hollis, August 28, 1820; his wife died October 6, 1798. Seven children born in Hollis.

- i. HANNAH, born September 7, 1772.
- ii. SALLY, born March 8, 1774; married January 24, 1793, Samuel Barron.
- iii. ALICE, born April 19, 1776.
- iv. MARY, born May 21, 1778; married November 10, 1797, Dea. Enos Hardy of Hollis.
- v. EPHRAIM, born August 14, 1780; died April 6, 1789.
- vi. STEPHEN, born October 29, 1783; married January 22, 1806, Rachel Shedd.
- vii. EBENEZER, born July 10, 1786.

13. MAJOR JOHN LUND, son of William, Jr. born February 22, 1749. He was a lieutenant in the Revolution and a major in the militia. He married March 26, 1772, Hannah Phelps. He died March 11, 1822. His widow died May 4, 1847, aged 96 years.

- i. SARAH, born June 30, 1772; married Cummings Pollard.
- ii. LUCY, born December 10, 1773; married Silas Read.
- iii. WILLIAM, born January 25, 1778; married Rebecca Clark.
- iv. HANNAH, born December 10, 1780; married Cummings Pollard.
- v. REBECCA, born December 10, 1780, twin.
- vi. MARY, born September 25, 1782; married S. I. Ettridge.
- vii. CLIFTON, born December 7, 1784; married June 13, 1815, Rebecca Carlton of Merrimack. He died April 26, 1857. She died November 6, 1869. John C. Lund, born in Nashua, 1821; died January 14, 1896, was their son.
- viii. JOHN, born December 1788, not married.
- ix. CLARISSA, born May, 1793; married Timothy Presby.
- x. JONATHAN, born September 17, 1796; married Rebecca Eaton.

1. PATRICK MARKS, whose age was 55 in 1685, resided in Charlestown several years. His wife, Sarah, was admitted to the church in Charlestown, April 10, 1687. The family removed to Dunstable in 1690. Scarcely had they made a home on the frontier before the Indians made an assault upon the settlement, and on the evening of September 2, 1691, they murdered three of the Hassell family and a daughter of Patrick Marks.

He was a surveyor of highways in 1690, and subsequently the name disappears in the records of the town. The town and church records of Charlestown give the names of five children.

  i. SARAH, born April 23, 1662.
  ii. PETER, born October 14, 1663; died November 20, 1663.
  iii. HANNAH, born October 5, 1664.
  iv. MERCIE, born February 5, 1667-8; admitted to the church in Charlestown, June 30, 1689.
  v. MARY, aged 18 years, was baptized in Charlestown, January 20, 1688-9. It is recorded at Dunstable: "Mary Marks, the daughter of Patrick Marks was slain by the Indians on September 2, in the evening Anno Domini 1691."

1. ROBERT PARRIS. This name is frequently written Parish. He was probably born before 1636. He lived in Groton, Massachusetts, from 1663 to 1676, when he removed to Dunstable. He was a soldier in King Philip's War, serving in Capt. Samuel Mosely's company, and at the garrison at Dunstable in 1676. Late in the same year he was appointed an assistant to Col. Jonathan Tyng, in the care of the friendly Indians who were supported by the province and colonized at Dunstable. He owned extensive tracts of land and was prominent in the councils of the town. The records are not complete but it is manifest that he was one of the selectmen, 1683, 1687, 1688, 1694, 1699, 1700, 1701, 1702, and in 1689 he was a representative. He was appointed from time to time on committees and joined with his townsmen in petitions to the General Court.

Before the close of Queen Anne's War he removed from Dunstable to Chelsea, Massachusetts, probably in the year 1705, and there died in 1709. In his will, dated August 21, 1709, and proved September 5, 1709, he is styled "Robert Parris formerly of the town of Dunstable, now living in Rumney Marsh." His wife, Elizabeth, was appointed executrix; to her he bequeathed a life use of his homestead and other lands in Dunstable. At her decease the same was "to be equally divided between my two daughters, Mary Richardson and Hannah Goff." There is no mention in the will of other children. There is mention of "fifty acres of land which my father John Blanchard gave to my wife in his will" and "fifty acres of land that her grandfather Hills gave to her in his will."

Thirty Dunstable Families. 57

Robert Parris married May 22, 1663, Seaborne (Bachelder) Cromwell, born in Charlestown, baptized March 12, 1634-5, daughter of William and Jane (Cowper) Bachelder, and widow of John Cromwell, see Cromwell family. He married, second, April 16, 1667, Mary Crispe, born Watertown, May 20, 1638, daughter of Benjamin and Bridget Crispe. He married, third, about 1685, Elizabeth Blanchard, daughter of Dea. John and Hannah (Hills) Blanchard of Dunstable. Elizabeth, widow of Robert Parris, married, second, 1710, Dea. Thomas Burrage, born May 26, 1663, son of John and Joanna (Stower) Burrage of Lynn. This was his second marriage; his first wife was Elizabeth Breed. Dea. Burrage was a prominent citizen of Lynn, where he died March 11, 1717-8. One child of Robert and Seaborne Parish was born in Groton. Five children of Robert and Mary Parish were born in Groton, and one in Dunstable.

   i. THOMAS, died April 18, 1668.

  ii. MERCY, born January 5, 1667-8. In record of birth the name is Mary. In subsequent records she is called Mercy. She married December 14, 1687, Josiah Richardson, born in Chelmsford, May 18, 1665, son of Josiah and Remembrance (Underwood) Richardson. They lived in Chelmsford, where he was a town clerk and selectman. He died November 21, 1711. She died April 25, 1743. They had six children. See Richardson Genealogy.

 iii. ANNA, born April 2, 1669; died June 8, 1671.

 iv. ROBERT, born November 20, 1670. Not named in the will of his father. Probably died young.

  v. ANNA, born September 10, 1672; died young.

 vi. MARY, born September 8, 1674; died young.

vii. HANNAH, born in Dunstable, 1679; married in Chelmsford, (date omitted in record,) John Goffe, born in Boston, September 18, 1679, son of John and Hannah (Sumner) Goffe. They removed from Boston to Londonderry, 1719. He died September 18, 1748. Four children. John born March 16, 1700-1701; married in Boston, October 16, 1722, Hannah Briggs. He was a colonel in the French and Indian War and one of the foremost men of his time; *Hannah*, born February 4, 1705-6, married February 9, 1723, Edward Linkfield; *Sarah*, born August 10, 1709, married Benjamin Kidder; *Mary*, born April 12, 1711; married 1737, Joseph Pearson; married, second, Woods.

NOTE—The story of the massacre of Robert Parris and his wife and daughter and the miraculous escape of two little daughters by an ingenious concealment in the cellar has been given in several publications. The event is not mentioned by Penhallow or by Pike. The story of the massacre was first published, 1823, in Farmer and Moore's Collections,

Vol. II, page 306. It has been refreshed and enlarged by Fox and Nason. The record proves that Robert Parris died in Chelsea and that his wife survived him. One of the little girls said to have been concealed in the cellar on the date of the assumed attack, was a wife and mother of several children and was safely living in Chelmsford; the other was married and living in Boston.

1. REV. SAMUEL PARRIS, son of Thomas Parris, came from Barbadoes to Boston about 1675. His father, Thomas, was a merchant in London and later in Barbadoes, where he died 1673. The son, Samuel, was a student at Harvard University, but did not graduate. He lived several years in Boston. He and his wife, Elizabeth, were members of the First Church, 1681 to 1689. In 1685 he preached in Stow, and at times he was a teacher in several towns in that vicinity. He was settled over the church of Salem Village, now Danvers, November 19, 1689. He and his wife were foundation members of that church. During his ministry at Salem Village, the witchcraft delusion, originating in his family, was the occasion of bitter persecution and a few cruel executions. The delusion was a concerted act, founded on an abnormal condition of the public mind. No one person originated it, nor could many wiser men stay its rage. Mr. Parris has been unjustly censured because a member of his family was the first person accused of witchcraft. During the excitement of the time, his ministry at Salem Village was terminated in 1696. Subsequently he lived several years in Watertown and Concord, where he was a trader and at times a licensed retailer. He began preaching in Dunstable in 1708, and preached here much of the time until 1712, and during these years he resided here. From this town he removed to Sudbury, living in the eastern part of the town, now Wayland. He was then a farmer, and at times a school teacher. He died February 27, 1719-20. His wife, Elizabeth, died at Salem Village, July 14, 1696. He married, second, Dorothy Noyes, a daughter of Peter and Elizabeth (Darrell) Noyes of Sudbury. She died September 6, 1719.

Three children of first and four of second wife.

    i. THOMAS, born, Boston, October 25, 1681; died young.

   ii. ELIZABETH, born Boston, November 28, 1682; married in Sudbury, January 13, 1709-10, Benjamin Barron, born about 1680, son of Ellis and Sarah (Ingersol) Barron of Watertown. They lived in Concord, where he died July 13, 1754; she died March 21, 1760. Five children born in Concord. Benjamin Barron, the husband of Elizabeth, was

Thirty Dunstable Families. 59

a brother of Ellis Barron of Lovewell's third expedition. In Bond's Watertown, page 391, he is erroneously called Benjamin Barnard.

iii. SUSANNAH, born, Boston, January 9, 1687-8; died at Concord, December 20, 1706.

iv. NOYES, born Watertown, August 22, 1699; Harvard University, 1721. He was a minister and for a short time chaplain at Castle William. Subsequently he preached in New Jersey. He died before 1750. He was not married.

v. DOROTHY, born Watertown, August 18, 1700; she married at Sudbury, November 25, 1718, Hopestill Brown, born at Sudbury, August 26, 1691, son of Hopestill and Abigail (Haynes) Brown. They lived in Sudbury, where she died March 4, 1724-5.

vi. SAMUEL, born, Watertown, January 9, 1701-2. He lived in East Sudbury, now Wayland. He was a deacon. His wife, Abigail, died February 15, 1759. He married, second, November 28, 1760, Abigail Fiske. Two children of first wife, *Samuel* and *Peter*, died young. The children of the second wife were: *Abigail*, born November 25, 1761, married Samuel Reeves of East Sudbury; *Dorothy*, born February 26, 1764, married Cheever Kendall and removed to Hope, Maine; Samuel, born December 28, 1767; married Mary Brown of Framingham.

vii. MARY, born, Concord, October 20, 1703; married April 18, 1727, Peter Bent, born May 17, 1703, son of Hopestill and Elizabeth (Brown) Bent of East Sudbury. Eleven children.

1. OBADIAH PERRY, son of William and Anna Perry of Watertown; married August 21, 1667, Esther Hassell, born Cambridge, December 6, 1648, daughter of Richard Hassell. See Hassell family. They lived a few years in Watertown and was one of the first families of Dunstable. On account of the exposure during King Philip's War, he removed to Concord and soon after, to Billerica. It is recorded in Billerica, "February 10, 1675-6, Obadiah Perry, belonging to Dunstable towne, now resident at Concord, but being inforced to remove from thence and not accounting it safe at ye present to remove to his owne at Dunstable, desiring at present to hire a house at Billerica, the selectmen, considering his condition, do grant him liberty to hire in this towne."

He returned to Dunstable before 1680, and was there killed by the Indians, September 28, 1691. "Obadiah Perry and Christopher Temple dyed by the hand of our Indian enemies, September, the twenty eighth day in the morning." His widow, Esther, married second,

August 30, 1693, Martin Townsend of Watertown. He died 1698.

Record is found of six children of Obadiah and Esther (Hassell) Perry.

   i. OBADIAH, born, Watertown, October 11, 1669.

   ii. EBENEZER, born, Watertown, November 20, 1671.

   iii. ESTHER, born, Watertown, August 11, 1674; married at Concord, May 11, 1692, to William Harwood. (See Harwood family.)

   iv. SAMUEL, born, Billerica, July 19, 1677; died November 25, 1677.

   v. JOHN, born, Dunstable, January 31, 1682.

   vi. ELIZABETH, born, Dunstable, April 7, 1683.

CHRISTOPHER READ, the tanner, lived in Dunstable a few years. If his residence here was brief, his name is firmly written into the early annals of the settlement. He was a selectman, was appointed on many committees and his signature appears on the petitions of his time. In 1672, he was a tanner of Boston, and was taxed in 1674 and presumably in other years. His wife, Katharine, was admitted to the Old South Church in 1673. In 1674, he removed to Cambridge and the same year he bought a homestead there. He was chosen a constable of Cambridge, November 12, 1677, collector January 13, 1678-9, surveyor November 12, 1683, tithingman March 17, 1683-4. He sold his homestead in Cambridge, June 20, 1685, and the same year removed to Dunstable, where he and John Lovewell, senior, were tanners. During the troublous times of King William's War, he removed from Dunstable to Boston, where he died 1696. Administration was granted to his widow, Katherine, September 3, 1696, and in the inventory of his estate was a house and land in Dunstable, under mortgage to Peter Town of Cambridge. In 1710, on the petition of Elizabeth Whiting, who says she is the wife of Samuel Whiting of Dunstable and the only child of Christopher Read, deceased, Col. Joseph Varnum of Dracut was appointed administrator to sell two hundred acres of land in Dracut, belonging to estate of the late Christopher Read.

Katherine, widow of Christopher Read, married second, William Green of Groton. The intention of marriage, in Boston, November 19, 1696. In 1710 she was deceased.

i. ELIZABETH, married in Dunstable, January 27, 1686-7, Samuel Whiting, see.

THOMAS READ, a tailor of Chelmsford was born about 1656; parentage unknown. He was not a son of Obadiah and Anna Read, as stated in Read Genealogy, 1861. He was a freeman, April 1, 1679, and a soldier in King Philip's War, 1676. He married, probably in 1679, Hannah Blanchard, daughter of Dea. John and Elizabeth (Hills) Blanchard, see. On the warrant of warning or caution against settlement in Chelmsford issued June 10, 1679, under date of June 14, 1679, the constable made a return: "Thomas Read and Hannah Read, his wife, is fled away out of our town we know not whither," and a second return dated September 27, 1679, the constable says: "Thomas Rade and hanna Blanchar are run away out of this county and I am informed they are gone to the southward." If he lived elsewhere a number of years it is certain that he returned to Chelmsford. In 1717, he sold to Joseph Blanchard of Dunstable the land willed to his wife, Hannah, by her grandfather, Joseph Hills, and by her father, Dea. John Blanchard. In 1725, the selectmen of Chelmsford petition the General Court, saying Thomas Blanchard "an ancient and infirm man" had petitioned the town for assistance and that his sons John, Thomas, William and Jonathan, who were able, had refused to assist him. Very probably Thomas and Hannah (Blanchard) Read had more children than are named in this register.

  i. JOHN, born 1685; married January 10, 1706, Jane Chamberlain; lived in Westford, where ten children were born.

  ii. THOMAS, born 1687; married March 14, 1709-10, Sarah Fletcher; lived in Westford, where he died December 24, 1773. He was prosperous and respected. Of their children, *Timothy* is named hereafter. The late Elbridge Gerry Reed is a descendant.

  iii. WILLIAM, married Hannah Bates of Chelmsford. He lived in Westford. His son, *Robert*, born December 25, 1720, married May 11, 1743, Mary Abbot of Andover, and was a leading citizen of Litchfield and Amherst. His second son, *William*, born February 25, 1724-5, married Lucy Spalding. He settled in the north part of Litchfield. He was an ensign in Col. Gilman's regiment, 1755, and was commissioned a captain soon after. He established a ferry between Litchfield and Merrimack, about 1728, known as "Read's Ferry." He died 1768, being killed at the raising of a building. In 1789, the legislature made a grant of a ferry to his son, William Read.

62   Thirty Dunstable Families.

  iv. JONATHAN. married Margaret. Two children born in Westford.
  v. BENJAMIN, born October 23, 1698; died in Westford, April 2, 1778.

2. TIMOTHY READ, son of Thomas and Sarah (Fletcher) Read, born in Westford, March 21, 1714. He married November 10, 1732, Mary Cummings, born July 5, 1708, daughter of John and Elizabeth (Adams) Cummings. He removed to Groton. His homestead was in Joint Grass district which in 1753 was annexed to Dunstable, Mass. His wife died November 3, 1778; he died April 26, 1799. Six children.

  i. ELIZABETH, born Westford, February 2, 1732-3.
  ii. MARY, born, Westford, February 22, 1734-5.
  iii. TIMOTHY, born, Westford, August 30, 1736; married Susannah Perham. Lived in Dunstable, Mass. Their children were *Susannah, Sybel, Timothy, Isaac, Mary, Rebecca, Catherine, William, James,* and *Sybel.*
  iv. CATHERINE, born, Groton, May 1, 1738.
  v. MARTHA, born, Groton, May 9, 1742; died January 20, 1758.
  vi. ELEAZER, born, Groton, February, 1749; married January 1, 1771, Rachel Cummings. He died in Dunstable, Mass., August 10, 1811. She died February 28, 1828, aged 87. Children: *Rachel, Rhoda, Caleb, Leonard, Rebecca,* and *Betty.*

1. LIEUT. JONATHAN ROBBINS. son of George and Alice Robbins, was born in Chelmsford, November 19, 1686. He was a brother of Lieut. Eleazer Robbins of Groton and Harvard. He came from Chelmsford to Dunstable about 1708, and soon purchased land and settled at Long Hill. He was one of the petitioners for leave to organize an independent company to scout against the Indians and was commissioned a lieutenant. He served under Capt. Lovewell in the three memorable expeditions. Early in the engagement May 8, 1725, he was mortally wounded and died on the field of battle.

  Lieut. Jonathan Robbins married at Concord, January 16, 1711-12, Margaret Lund, a daughter of Thomas Lund of Dunstable. In the record of marriage they are styled "of Dunstable." The same day at Concord, Thomas Lund of Dunstable, a brother of Margaret, married Elizabeth Taylor of Concord. See Lund family. Margaret (Lund) Robbins married, second, 1729, William Shattuck, born 1689, son of William and Hannah

(Underwood) Shattuck. They lived at Groton, where he died in August, 1754. She died June 13, 1764. Five children of Lieut. Jonathan and Margaret Robbins, born at Dunstable. Three children of William and Margaret Shattuck born in Groton.

i. JANE, born December 26, 1712; married at Groton, April 14, 1731, Stephen Ames, born at Boxford, September 1, 1712, son of John and Priscilla (Kimball) Ames. The Ames family removed to Groton in 1717, and there John Ames, the father, was killed by the Indians, July 24, 1726. Stephen Ames lived in Groton until 1740, when he removed to Hollis. Three children were born in Groton and four in Hollis.

ii. MARGARET, born February 29, 1715.

iii. JONATHAN, born November 4, 1718.

iv. ELEANOR, born June 8, 1721; married James Whitney, born 1714, son of Joseph and Rebecca (Burge) Whitney. They lived in Dunstable where he died, 1755. A daughter, Eleanor, born July 23, 1740, married Frances Pollard; a son, James, born November 4, 1742, married Sarah Lund.

v. ELIZABETH, born September 20, 1723.

vi. EZEKIEL SHATTUCK, born, Groton, June 12, 1730, a soldier in the French and Indian War, he died in the service, 1758.

vii. MARGARET SHATTUCK, born July 4, 1732; married May 26, 1752, Joseph Bennett, born December 15, 1725, son of Benjamin and Mary (Lakin) Bennett. He died soon, and their only child died in infancy. She married, second, January 24, 1759, Joseph Metcalf. He was a soldier in the French and Indian War. He lived in Groton until 1770, when he removed to Ashburnham, where he died March 19, 1793. She died June 20, 1802. They were worthy and esteemed and their descendants are capable and useful. Nine children.

viii. JOB SHATTUCK, born February 11, 1736. He was a soldier in the French and Indian War. In the Revolution he was engaged at Lexington and Bunker Hill. Subsequently he was commissioned a captain, serving with zeal and marked ability in 1776, 1777, and 1779. He was involved in Shays' rebellion and had the courage and ability to become conspicuous. He was arrested, tried and sentenced to be hanged. His unblemished character and his former good service to his town and to the state could not be set aside and he was pardoned. Subsequently he enjoyed the confidence and respect of his townsmen. Job Shattuck married May 25, 1758, Sarah Hartwell, born at Groton, March 19, 1738, daughter of Samuel and Sarah (Holden) Hartwell. She died, May 5, 1798. He married, second, May 26, 1800, Elizabeth (Lakin) Gragg, daughter of William and Miriam (Erwin) Lakin and widow of John Gragg of Groton. He died in Groton, January 13, 1819. His widow died June 1, 1824. Of Job and Sarah (Hartwell) Shattuck there were nine children.

1. SAMUEL SEARLES, son of Col. Daniel and Deliverance (Tyng) Searles, was born at Boston, October 16, 1668. His father, Col. Daniel Searles, was well connected in Boston and prominent in public affairs. He was Governor of Barbadoes, 1652-1660, and there he resided many years. His mother was a daughter of Hon. Edward and a sister of Hon. Jonathan Tyng. Samuel Searles came to Dunstable before 1699, and it is probable that in his youth he had a home with his uncle, Jonathan Tyng. He was one of the foremost men of the town and was actively engaged in the land speculations of his time. He died before 1737. He married September 26, 1699, Sarah Perham. Widow Sarah Searles was taxed 1738.

  i. SARAH, born October 20, 1700.
  ii. DELIVERANCE, born January 10, 1702.
2. iii. SAMUEL, born March 1, 1707.
  iv. MARY, born October 10, 1710.
3. v. DANIEL born July 17, 1715.
4. vi. JOHN, born October 11, 1717.
5. vii. JONATHAN, born September 5, 1720.

2. SAMUEL SEARLES, son of Samuel, born March 1, 1707. He married January 17, 1737, Mary Butterfield, born 1711, daughter of Benjamin and Sarah Butterfield. He lived in Dunstable. His wife died October 24, 1754. He died January 8, 1758.

6. i. SAMUEL, born September 2, 1738.
  ii. BENJAMIN, born September 4, 1740; died January 27, 1756.
  iii. MARY, born January 10, 1744.

3. DANIEL SEARLES, son of Samuel, born Dunstable, July 17, 1715. He lived in Dunstable, where four or more children were born. His wife was Mary.

  i. OLIVER, born August 20, 1736; died September 8, 1738.
  ii. JAMES, born November 17, 1738.
  iii. RACHEL, born March 1, 1746.
  iv. LUCY, born March 10, 1754.

4. JOHN SEARLES, son of Samuel, born Dunstable, October 11, 1717. He lived in Dunstable. The birth of five children is on record.

Thirty Dunstable Families. 65

- i. LUCY, born March 10, 1754; died February 7, 1774.
- ii. SARAH, born October 10, 1757.
- iii. ESTHER, born July 16, 1760.
- iv. LYDIA, born October 29, 1762.
- v. JOTHAM, born May 8, 1765, see History of Francestown.

5. JONATHAN SEARLES, son of Samuel, born September 21, 1720. He married at Westford, October 12, 1748, Thankful Bixby, born 1725, daughter of David and Abigail Bixby. He settled in Hudson. He died 1786.
   - i. THANKFUL, born May 23, 1750.
   - ii. JONATHAN, born April 11, 1752.
   - iii. THOMAS, born August 28, 1754.
   - iv. JACOB, born April 15, 1757.
   - v. ELIHU, born September 28, 1759.
   - vi. ELNATHAN, born March 26, 1763.
   - vii. LYDIA, born July 1, 1765.

6. SAMUEL SEARLES, son of Samuel, Jr., born September 2, 1738. He lived in Dunstable; married 1759, Elizabeth. He died about 1786. His wife survived him.
   - i. CATE, born April 16, 1760.
   - ii. ELIZABETH, born January 13, 1762.
   - iii. SAMUEL, born April 23, 1764.
   - iv. BENJAMIN, born February 22, 1766.
   - v. JAMES, born July 28, 1767.
   - vi. HENRY ADAMS, born March 27, 1769.
   - vii. KATHERINE, born February 25, 1774.

1. BENJAMIN SMITH in 1731 petitioned the General Court of Massachusetts for the two islands in the Merrimack river and for land on the west bank of the river opposite the islands. The General Court, June 20, 1733 "in consideration of his great services for the province in divers marches against the Indian enemy" and because "he has presumed to take up about sixteen acres partly on an island about a mile above Souhegan river and partly on the main land adjacent thereto and has built a house thereon" granted him the two islands and sufficient land on the west bank of the Merrimack river to make fifty acres. See N. H. State Papers, Vol. XXIV, page 13. Bedford originally called Narragansett No. 5,

was granted February 12, 1733-4. The original grant, extending south to the Souhegan river, included the north half of the present town of Merrimack, and allowance was made in the grant for the farm of Benjamin Smith, which was situated within the township. He was chosen by the proprietors of Bedford, January 25, 1738, one of a committee to lay a road between the first and second range of lots, and October 19, 1743, Col. John Goffe, Moses Barron and Benjamin Smith were instructed to perambulate the town lines.

He was the first settler in that vicinity but the exact date of his arrival cannot be stated. Dating from the grant of Bedford, which included his grant, he had lived in that town sixteen years when the southern part of Bedford, including his grant, was annexed to Merrimack. In present terms the grant to Benjamin Smith was at Reed's Ferry, and the two islands in the river are now of the same contour and area as they were in 1731.

Benjamin Smith died in 1750. The inventory of his estate is dated October 14, 1750, the amount of his real and personal property was above the average of his time. Among the one hundred and thirty-two items of inventory are included lands, buildings, a ferry boat, Indian corn, English grain, hay, horses, oxen, cows, young cattle, guns, traps, linen wheels, feather beds and all the appointments of a farm and a well furnished home.

Benjamin Smith probably was married when he settled at Reed's Ferry in Merrimack, before 1731, but a record of his marriage and of his children, if any by a first marriage, has not been discovered. He married soon after 1728, Mrs. Hannah Lovewell, widow of Capt. John Lovewell, the hero of Pigwacket. To them one child, Elizabeth, was born in Bedford, April 10, 1744.

Thus Benjamin Smith became the step-father of, and under his parental care were reared, the three children of Capt. John and Hannah Lovewell. In March, 1751, Samuel Wadsworth, clerk of the proprietors of Bedford, made a list of the improved lots of the township, including the part of Merrimack lying north of Souhegan river. Among the occupants of farms named in the list is found the name of "Widow Smith once Capt. lovels widow" The date of her death is not known. Fox's Dunstable says she died January 5, 1754, but it was the mother, not the widow of Capt.

Thirty Dunstable Families. 67

John Lovewell, who died January 5, 1754. There was a Dea. Benjamin Smith, a younger man, who came from Londonderry to Bedford about 1745, and died there 1812, but there was no connection between the two men of the same name.

1. AMBROSE SWALLOW, the ancestor of the Swallow families of New Hampshire and Massachusetts, was an early resident of Chelmsford. He married December 2, 1668, Mary Martin. In the return of the marriage to the county his name is written Ambrose fearlon. This very probably is an error in transcribing. His name is uniformly written Ambrose Swallow in the records of Chelmsford and in probate record. He died in Chelmsford, October 25, 1684. His wife, Mary, married, second, Samuel Warner of Dunstable, see.

   The inventory of his estate, dated November 3, 1684, amounts to £230-17-6, and includes "His homelott within fence with orchard & housing on same; His old field and land adjoining; His meadow Billerica bounds; His Spring meadow & upland adjacent; 5 cows, 2 oxen, 1 heifer, 2 calves, 1 horse, 18 swine, 2 bibles & other books, arms, ammunition, 5 Bbls Cyder, flax, hemp, yarn, & Tobacco &c."

   In the inventory it is stated that Ambrose Swallow died October 20, 1684. In town records the date of his death is October 25, 1684.

   Four children of Ambrose and Mary Martin Swallow:

   2. i. AMBROSE, born September 8, 1669.
   3. ii. JOHN, born November 19. 1671.
   4. iii. JOSEPH, born March 16, 1679.
   5. iv. BENJAMIN, born November 9, 1683.

2. AMBROSE SWALLOW, son of Ambrose, born in Chelmsford, September 8, 1669. He lived in Chelmsford. He married, December 8, 1696, Sarah Barrett, probably a daughter of John and Sarah Barrett. He died April 19, 1720. Land in the second division was granted, January 12, 1720-1, to Sarah Swallow in the right of Ambrose Swallow, deceased. She died November 22, 1756. Six children.

   i. SARAH, born July 23, 1698.
   ii. MARY, born February 8, 1700; died May 25, 1716.
   iii. HANNAH, born January 18, 1703.

68   *Thirty Dunstable Families.*

 6. iv. JONATHAN, born September 11, 1706.
 7. v. JOHN, born August 2, 1709.
 8. vi. JOSEPH, born June 21, 1714.

3. JOHN SWALLOW, son of Ambrose, born November 19, 1671. He married January 3, 1693, Anna Barrett, born December 17, 1668, daughter of Thomas and Frances (Woolderson) Barrett of Chelmsford. Thomas Barrett with consent of Mary, a second wife, for love and affection, July 8, 1700, conveys to his son, John Swallow, a house and thirty acres of upland and meadow. Anna, wife of John Swallow, died in Chelmsford, May 10, 1735. He died May 27, 1756..

4. JOSEPH SWALLOW, son of Ambrose, born March 19, 1679. He was a wheelwright and early in life he settled in Reading, Mass. He married 1713, Abigail Upton, born 1697, daughter of Joseph and Abigail Upton. His homestead was in the part of the town now North Reading, where he died 1755. By will he gives his estate, real and personal, to his wife, Abigail. She died 1781. Her will is dated May 29, 1781. "For his faithfulness and friendship," she gives to "Stephen Buxton, Jr., with whom I reside"; other bequests are made to Phebe, wife of Stephen Buxton, Jr., to Sarah Graves, to her sister, Mehitable (Upton) Wilkins, wife of Hezekiah Wilkins and to Mary Buxton and Dorcas Upton.

5. BENJAMIN SWALLOW, son of Ambrose, born in Chelmsford, November 9, 1683. He was an infant when his widowed mother married Samuel Warner of Dunstable. He settled in Groton, where he purchased several tracts of land, the deeds bearing dates from 1729 to 1758. His homestead was in the north part of the town. In 1739, he was one of the petitioners for a new town to include a part of Groton and a part of Dunstable, and in 1742, he joined with others for a division of Groton. This discussion culminated in the erection of the West Parrish, now Pepperell. He was the moderator of the first meeting of the parish and one of the prudential committee. He married in Concord, May 21, 1707, Elizabeth (Blood) Williams, born in Groton, October 7, 1673, daughter of Nathaniel and Hannah (Parker) Blood and widow of Thomas Williams. He married, second, November 20, 1746, Widow Hannah Green.

Hannah Swallow, wife of Benjamin Swallow, buys sixteen acres in Pepperell, September 30, 1754. No record of children is found.

February 19, 1720, Benjamin Swallow and wife, Elizabeth, convey to "our dutiful son Isaac Williams all the real estate in Middlesex county devised to said Elizabeth as one of the grandchildren of Capt. James Parker, deceased."

November 23, 1744, Benjamin Swallow and Isaac Williams convey to Jason Williams, Jr., and John Williams, certain lands in Groton and all rights in Groton Commons of Thomas Williams' wife and children, except those laid out to heirs of Thomas Williams, 2d, late deceased and one-fifth of the commons now due to Thomas Williams' wife and children.

6. JONATHAN SWALLOW, son of Ambrose, Jr., born in Chelmsford, September 11, 1706. He was a blacksmith in Chelmsford. December 30, 1730 he bought of John Corey, a house and forty acres. His wife, Hannah, died March 16, 1770. Seven children.

    i. ELIZABETH, born July 29, 1729; married April 10, 1755, Benjamin Wood.

    ii. HANNAH, born February 11, 1730-1; married January 7, 1754, Samuel Wilson.

    iii. JONATHAN, born May 7, 1734; died September 27, 1741.

    iv. MARY, born November 11, 1736.

    v. JONATHAN, born March 24, 1739-40.

    vi. PHEBE, born August 9, 1742; married October 4, 1764, David Parker, born June 3, 1745, son of Benjamin and Mary (Corey) Parker of Billerica.

    vii. EPHRAIM, born June 13, 1745; died September 30, 1749.

7. JOHN SWALLOW, son of Ambrose, Jr., born August 2, 1709. He settled in the north part of Groton. In 1753, his farm and other lands were annexed to Dunstable, Mass. He united with the church of Groton, October 29, 1732, and he and his wife, Sarah, were foundation members of the church of Dunstable, which was embodied May 12, 1757. He married Deborah, who was the mother of John and Amaziah. He married, second, Sarah Nutting, born, Groton, February 22, 1714-5, daughter of Jonathan and Mary (Green) Nutting. She was the mother of eight children. I have not found a record of either marriage. He died in Dunstable,

February 15, 1776. His widow, Sarah, died January 20, 1799.

9. i. JOHN, born February 22, 1729-30.
10. ii. AMAZIAH, born November 22, 1732.
   iii. BENJAMIN, born October 21, 1736; married March 5, 1767, Joanna Spalding, born in Westford, April 7, 1738, daughter of Andrew and Hannah Spalding. They lived in Dunstable, Mass. He was a soldier in the Revolution. He died January 11, 1821. His wife died November 22, 1820. They 3, 1775; *Joanna*, born September 22, 1781, and a son, had *David*, born November 5, 1771; *Joanna*, born January *Samson*, who lived several years, at least, in Dunstable. Two daughters of Samson were wives of Ira Spalding of Clinton, Maine.
   iv. SARAH, born November 25, 1741.
11. v. PETER, born October 9, 1743.
   vi. MARY, born February 28, 1746.
   vii. DEBORAH, born February 9, 1748; married December 14, 1769, David Woods, born Groton, December 31, 1746, son of John and Sarah (Longley) Woods. He died in Deering, N. H., 1793. She married, second, December 31, 1797, Amos Eastman of Hollis. She died March 7, 1821. He died August 2, 1832.
   viii. ELIZABETH, born December 17, 1750; married March 12, 1772, Samuel Roby. He died November 3, 1799; she died October 19, 1812. Six children.
   ix. HANNAH, born January 17, 1754.
   x. JONATHAN, born June 22, 1757; married at Westford, March 18, 1788, Jemima Wilson. He lived in Groton and in Dunstable, Mass. Their children were: *Alice; Lucinda; Jonathan*, born February 18, 1793; *Clarinda*, born 18, 1795; *Sophronia*, born January 30, 1799; *John Wilson*, born April 18, 1803; *Sarah*, born September 3, 1806.

8. JOSEPH SWALLOW, son of Ambrose, Jr., born June 21, 1714. He lived in Dunstable. He was an active man and a useful citizen, and was one of those who joined with the Blanchards in opposition to the settlement of Rev. Samuel Bird. He married Susannah Sanderson, who died about 1748. He married, second, 1751, Esther Robbins of Westford.

One child of the first and five of the second wife.

   i. JOSEPH, born August 6, 1746.
   ii. THOMAS, born July 30, 1753; died young.
   iii. SILAS, born July 25, 1754; married in Hollis, June 16, 1786, Lucy Emerson, born October 29, 1751, daughter of Rev. Daniel and Hannah (Emerson) Emerson. He was a

Thirty Dunstable Families. 71

worthy and esteemed citizen of Dunstable. He died February 26, 1846. Their son, *Joseph*, born June 30, 1787; married Betsey Twiss. They were the parents of Rev. Joseph Emerson Swallow.

iv. SUSANNAH, born March 4, 1756; married Phineas Whitney.

v. ESTHER, born April 29, 1759; married November 17, 1796, Jeremiah Hunt, born April 8, 1759, son of William and Mary (Hardy) Hunt.

vi. THOMAS, born August 1, 1760.

9. JOHN SWALLOW, son of John, born Groton, February 22, 1729-30. He lived in Mason, N. H., where he died November 23, 1815. He married November 19, 1755, Sarah Lawrence, who died December 28, 1763. He married, second, December 11, 1765, Mary Hall, born March 9, 1746, daughter of Nathan and Mary (Chapman) Hall of Mason. She died August 14, 1822. Four children of first and eleven of second wife, born in Mason.

i. JOHN, born January 3, 1757; married Rebecca Dunster, born June 18, 1756, daughter of Jason and Rebecca (Cutter) Dunster. He lived in Mason. He died in January, 1830. His wife died, August 3, 1811. Seven children.

ii. SARAH, born October 2, 1758.

iii. LYDIA, born October 31, 1760.

iv. DEBORAH, born November 15, 1762; married March 27, 1785, Noah Winship.

v. MOLLIE, born December 14, 1766; married October 22, 1786, Samuel Green.

vi. ABEL, born May 31, 1768; married October 21, 1794, Rachel Spalding. Lived in Groton.

vii. JOEL, born May 14, 1770.

viii. SYBEL, born April 6, 1772; married January 14, 1799, Josiah Winship.

ix. EUNICE, born July 3, 1774; died December 3, 1774.

x. EUNICE, born December 1, 1775; married December 27, 1798, Ezra Newell.

xi. DANIEL, born July 3, 1778. He was of Groton, 1799.

xii. AZUBAH, born August 7, 1780; married December 23, 1810, Samuel Withington.

xiii. RHODA, born June 17, 1783; married September 3, 1809, Elijah Knapp.

xiv. BETSEY, born February 18, 1786; married November 18, 1817, Artemas Rowell.

xv. DORCAS, born July 2, 1788; married April 22, 1816, Francis Humphries.

10. LIEUT. AMAZIAH SWALLOW, son of John, born November 22, 1732. He was a lieutenant of the Revolution and an officer of the militia. He lived in Groton and in Dunstable. His homestead was severed from Groton and annexed to Dunstable, February 25, 1793. He was a respected citizen. He died in Dunstable, Mass., January 21, 1803. He married in Billerica, June 19, 1759, Elizabeth Kendall, born February 14, 1739, died December 9, 1784. He married, second, February 16, 1786, Mary (Taylor) Woods, born January 17, 1749-50 daughter of Samuel and Susannah (Perham) Taylor and widow of Capt. Solomon Woods. She died February 15, 1828. Nine children of the first and one of the second wife.

    i. ELIZABETH, born May 18, 1760; married June 25, 1789, Lieut. John Cheney.

    ii. REBECCA, born December 4, 1763; died August 17, 1765.

    iii. RUTH, born July 22, 1765; married September 13, 1785, Isaac Kendall.

12.   iv. ASA, born May 1, 1767.

    v. REBECCA, born April 24, 1768; married September 25, 1789, Jeremiah Cummings. Eight children.

13.   vi. ABRAHAM, born December 14, 1770.

    vii. DEBORAH, born December 14, 1773; died October 18, 1778.

    viii. KENDALL, born April 2, 1775; died October 25, 1778.

    ix. MARY, born November 30, 1777; died November 7, 1798.

14.   x. AMAZIAH, born 1787.

11. PETER SWALLOW, son of John, born October 9, 1743; married in Groton, February 8, 1770, Prudence Stiles, born at Lunenburg, April 3, 1747, daughter of Jacob and Sarah (Hartwell) Stiles. She died at Dunstable, March 20, 1780. He married, second, Sybel Blood. He was a soldier in the Revolution. He lived in Dunstable, Mass. He died April 7, 1813. Five children of first and five of second wife.

    i. NAHUM, born June 23, 1771; married December 22, 1796, Diademia Woods, born at Groton, October 28, 1778, daughter of Capt. Solomon and Mary (Taylor) Woods. He removed to Windsor, Vt., where he died January 15, 1851; Diademia died at Whitehall, Illinois, September 5, 1858. Eleven of their fifteen children removed to Illinois and Michigan.

    ii. PRUDENCE, born July 26, 1773; married November 22, 1792, Temple Kendall, born Dunstable, Mass., May 28, 1768, son

Thirty Dunstable Families. 73

of Temple and Abigail Kendall. He died August 20, 1850. She died January 6, 1868. Fourteen children.

- iii. LARNED, born July 30, 1775; died 1776.
- iv. LARNED, born June 18, 1777; married Olive Fletcher Proctor. Removed to Buckfield, Maine. Fifteen children.
- v. SARAH, born February 17, 1780.
- vi. ARCHELAUS, born January 10, 1784; married Susanna Kendall. He lived on the paternal homestead. Six children.
- vii. JAMES, born October 23, 1785.
- viii. LUCY, born November 10, 1787.
- ix. MOODY, born November 5, 1789.
- x. ABIJAH, born August 19, 1792.

12. ASA SWALLOW, son of Capt. Amaziah, born May 1, 1767. Married in Pepperell, June 29, 1791, Susannah Kendall, who died, leaving one son, 1792; he married, second, January 16, 1794, Susannah Woods, born November 12, 1772, daughter of Capt. Solomon and Mary (Taylor) Woods. He lived in Dunstable, Mass. He died February 15, 1813; she died April 27, 1848. Seven children.

- i. KENDALL, born June 14, 1792.
- ii. SUSANNAH, born September 23, 1794.
- iii. ASA, born April 3, 1796.
- iv. LAURA, born July 25, 1798.
- v. RUEL, born October 11, 1801.
- vi. BERA, born April 10, 1806.
- vii. MARIA, born January 6, 1811.

13. ABRAHAM SWALLOW, son of Lieut. Amaziah, born December 14, 1770; married December 23, 1790, Anna Blodgett. He lived in Dunstable, Mass. He was a town officer and a captain in the militia.

- i. RHODA, born September 30, 1791.
- ii. ABRAHAM, born January 19, 1795.
- iii. MARY, born May 20, 1797.
- iv. CALVIN, born April 20, 1799.
- v. LUTHER, born May 18, 1801.
- vi. SARAH, born August 31, 1803.

14. CAPT. AMAZIAH SWALLOW, son of Lieut. Amaziah, born 1787. He married January 18, 1810, Asenath Cummings, born July 26, 1788, daughter of Simeon and

Sarah Cummings. He was a captain in the militia and an intelligent, useful citizen. He died October 6, 1857. His widow died October 30, 1865. Six children.

    i. ALMIRA, born December 23, 1810; married Andrew Sawtelle.

    ii. ASENATH, born September 13, 1812; married April 1, 1833, Thomas Parker.

    iii. SARAH CUMMINGS, born September 7, 1815; married August 19, 1834, Albert Gallatin Page, born March 13, 1814, son of Edmund and Betsey (Dwight) Page of Dunstable. Mr. Page lived in Fitchburg, Mass. He was active in business and was one of the founders of the Whitman and Barnes Manufacturing Company, now of Akron, Ohio. He died March 27, 1871. Frank Dwight Page, city auditor of Fitchburg is a son of Albert G., and Sarah (Swallow) Page.

    iv. AMAZIAH NEWTON, born May 5, 1820; married June 23, 1852, Rebecca P. Proctor. He was a grocer of Charlestown, Mass.

    v. ALBERT ORSON, born December 12, 1822; died October 18, 1826.

    vi. ALBERT JOSIAH, born June 13, 1828; died December 7, 1850.

1. ABRAHAM TAYLOR, son of Abraham and Mary (Whitaker) Taylor and grandson of William Taylor of Concord, was born in Concord, January 11, 1682-3. He married December 9, 1706, Sarah Pellet, born in Concord, September 5, 1685, daughter of Thomas and Mary (Dane) Pellet. He lived in Concord until 1710, and there two sons were born. His wife, Sarah, died about the date of his removal to Dunstable. His second wife was Mary, but a record of the marriage is not found. He was a man of good character and a worthy citizen. His children were:

    i. ABRAHAM, born at Concord, April 4, 1707. He lived in Hollis and was a potent factor in the organization of the town. He gave the land for the meetinghouse, common and cemetery. He died June 3, 1743. He had sons, *Leonard* and *Abraham*, and daughters, *Lydia, Olive, Sarah* and *Submit.*

2.   ii. SAMUEL, born at Concord, October 1, 1708.

    iii. JOSEPH, baptized at Dunstable, September 13, 1716, by Rev. Caleb Trowbridge of Groton.

3.   iv. TIMOTHY, born September 1, 1718.

    v. ALICE, born April 15, 1720; married about 1750, Ebenezer Butterfield, born July 13, 1706, son of Samuel and Rachel (Spalding) Butterfield. It was his second marriage.

    vi. AMOS, born September 10, 1725; married May 21, 1747, Bridget Martin. He lived in Dunstable, in New Ipswich and in Hollis, removing to Brookline in 1772. He or his son, Amos, was a soldier of Capt. Reuben Dow's company of Col. Prescott's regiment at Bunker Hill and siege of Boston, 1775. In 1776, he removed to Stoddard. He had six or more children. *Amos*, born at Dunstable, September 7, 1748; *Edmund*, born at Dunstable, May 4, 1750, he settled in Cavendish, Vermont; *Ephraim*, not married, lived with the Harvard Shakers several years; *Bridget, Abraham, Isaac.*

2. SAMUEL TAYLOR, son of Abraham, was born at Concord, October 1, 1708. In his infancy the family removed to Dunstable. He lived in the southern part of the township, now Dunstable, Massachusetts. He was a man of good works, a useful citizen and for thirty-five years a deacon of the church. He died October 23, 1792. He married Susannah Perham, who died October 14, 1798. Eleven children.

   i. SAMUEL, born October 13, 1734. He was a soldier in the French and Indian War and died at Lake George, November 18, 1755.

   ii. REUBEN, born March 8, 1735-6; married Lucy Boutelle and settled in New Ipswich.

   iii. SUSANNAH, born November 28, 1737.

4. iv. JONAS, born November 30, 1739.

   v. LUCY, born April 4, 1742; married February 9, 1764, Jonathan Fletcher, born March 30, 1741, son of Joseph and Elizabeth (Underwood) Fletcher of Dunstable. He was a a captain in the militia, 1781. He died in Dunstable, Mass., March 30, 1813. She died July 17, 1301. Twelve children.

   vi. THADDEUS, born April 10, 1744; married Bridget Walton, born in Reading, Mass., May 29, 1746, daughter of John and Martha (Burnap) Walton. He removed from Dunstable to New Ipswich, where he died 1825. He is the ancestor of a numerous and worthy family. One of his sons was *Oliver Swain Taylor*, born December 17, 1784, Dartmouth College, 1809, preceptor, New Ipswich Appleton Academy and subsequently a physician of Auburn, New York.

   vii. OLIVER, born June 1, 1746; married July 16, 1767, Bridget Blodgett, born December 31, 1746, daughter of Josiah and Jemima (Nutting) Blodgett of Dunstable. His wife died January 15, 1794. He married, second, December 30, 1794, Abigail Richardson, born, Temple, June 14, 1775, daughter of Thomas and Abigail Richardson. He died October 13, 1823. Abigail, his widow, died January 19, 1839. Eight children by first and two by second marriage.

   viii. RACHEL, born May 11, 1748; died February 17, 1754.

   ix. MARY, born January 17, 1749.

Thirty Dunstable Families.

    x. ISAAC, born January 13, 1753; married November 21, 1776, Sarah Parkhurst, who died March 10, 1813. He married, second, 1814, Lucy Hill, born in Billerica, January 14, 1756, daughter of Jonathan and Mary (Lane) Hill. She died February 5, 1832.

    xi. SAMUEL, born March 20, 1756; married 1777, Ruth Parker, born in Groton, October 18, 1757, daughter of William and Ruth (Boynton) Parker. He removed to Milford; where he resided twenty-five years. He returned to Dunstable, Mass., and there died January 9, 1841. His wife died December 30, 1837. Eight children.

    xii. WILLIAM, born November 9, 1759; died May 6, 1771.

3. TIMOTHY TAYLOR, son of Abraham, was born at Dunstable, September 1, 1718. He married Rachel Converse, born in Merrimack, April 30, 1730, daughter of Joshua and Rachel (Blanchard) Converse. He lived in Merrimack; was a selectman and a prominent citizen. They had seven children born in Merrimack.

    i. MARY, born December 14, 1751.
5.   ii. TIMOTHY, born September 18, 1754.
    iii. JOSHUA, born September 18, 1756.
    iv. SARVIA, born August 27, 1758.
    v. ELEAZER, born April 17, 1760.
    vi. ABIGAIL, born March, 1762.
    vii. JOEL, born March 4, 1764.

4. JONAS TAYLOR, son of Abraham, born in Dunstable, November 30, 1739; married Mary Danforth, born February 5, 1745, daughter of Lieut. Joseph and Mary (Richardson) Danforth. He lived in Dunstable, Massachusetts, where he died December 15, 1823. She died December 5, 1813. Six children.

    i. JONAS, born 1767; died July 24, 1848; married Hannah, who died May 24, 1849.
    ii. DANFORTH, born October 30, 1769; he died in Stoddard, January 4, 1858.
    iii. MARY, born May 26, 1773.
    iv. ABIGAIL, born February 12, 1775.
    v. ABIGAIL, born May 30, 1780.
    vi. JACOB, born January 16, 1783.

5. TIMOTHY TAYLOR, son of Timothy, was born in Merrimack, September 18, 1754. He married in Merrimack, February 1, 1776, Esther (French) Toothaker,

born in Dunstable, 1754, daughter of Capt. Benjamin and Molley (Lovewell) French and widow of Dr. Allin Toothaker, a young physician of Merrimack, who died July 12, 1775. Timothy Taylor lived in Merrimack many years; he was a selectman 1780, 1784, 1785; representative 1785, 1787, 1788, 1790, 1793. He was a magistrate many years. In the legislature he was a useful and influential man, and in town affairs he was a foremost citizen. He removed from Merrimack to Dunstable, 1806, and in 1819 to Norwalk, Ohio, where he died February 26, 1851. His wife died July 1, 1843

i. GEORGE ALLIN, born February 16, 1777.

ii. ESTHER, born June 9, 1781; married December 30, 1804, Samuel Preston, born in New Ipswich, July 21, 1778, son of Dr. John and Rebecca (Farrar) Preston. Samuel Preston succeeded Samuel Cushing in the publication of the *Village Messenger* at Amherst. In 1801, he removed to Dunstable and was engaged in trade about eight years. Subsequently he lived in Norwalk, Ohio, where he died March 3, 1852. His wife died September 3, 1826. One son, *Charles Albert Preston.* Their daughter, *Lucy Bancroft Preston*, married January 15, 1835, Frederick Wickham.

iii. FANNIE, married ―――― Knight. They had one daughter, and sons, *James, George, William* and *Albert.*

iv. GILMAN, removed to Illinois.

v. BENJAMIN, by wife, Juliette, had *Catherine, Isabella, Catherine* and *Gilman.*

6. JONATHAN TAYLOR, son of Abraham and Mary (Whitaker) Taylor, was born in Concord, August 10, 1694. He removed to Dunstable about 1720. His wife, the mother of ten children was Hannah. A record of his marriage has not been discovered. He died 1748.

i. DAVID, born January 1, 1722-3; married April 16, 1752, Hannah Fletcher. She died October 23, 1800; he died December 15, 1809. Five children: *Hannah,* born May 23, 1753; *Sybel,* born April 9, 1755; *Catherine,* born September 3, 1757; *Olive,* born November 9, 1760, married June 17, 1802, Capt. Josiah Cummings, born June 12, 1763, son of Oliver and Sybel (Bailey) Cummings. She died November 24, *Sarah,* born January 9, 1764, married January 17, 1785, Capt. Josiah Cummings. She died January 24, 1802. He died September 11, 1834.

ii. ISRAEL, born February 23, 1723-4; died August 24, 1724.

iii. JONATHAN, born September 8, 1725; died young.

iv. EPHRAIM, twin, born September 8, 1725; died young.

- v. HANNAH, born January 19, 1727-8.
- vi. ESTHER, born January 8, 1729-30.
- vii. SARAH, born May 14, 1732.
- viii. NATHAN, born October 9, 1734.
- ix. OLIVE, born April 6, 1737; married, 1769, Abraham Clark of Townsend.
- x. SAMSON, born December 6, 1739; died young.
- xi. DANIEL.
- xii. JASON.
- xiii. MARY.

7. JOHN TAYLOR, perhaps a son of Abraham of Concord and brother of Abraham of Dunstable, born in Concord, September 8, 1685. He married in Charlestown, March 23, 1710, Sarah Cummings, born about 1692. She is not found in either of the two Cummings Genealogies, but probate records of the estate of Ebenezer Cummings present evidence that she was his sister and a daughter of John and Elizabeth (Kinsley) Cummings. He settled on the east side of the Merrimack river and was living in a garrison when Nottingham was incorporated in 1733. His homestead was one-half mile east of the river and one mile north of Taylor's Falls bridge. There is no record of his death. Six children were born in Dunstable.

- i. ELIZABETH, born December 30, 1710; married Benjamin Hassell, see. Lived in Merrimack.
- ii. HANNAH, born March 29, 1713.
- iii. SARAH, born March 7, 1715.
- iv. EUNICE, born October 31, 1717; married Jeremiah Carleton, son of Joseph and Abigail (Osgood) Carleton of Newbury, Mass. They lived in Litchfield and Lyndeborough.
- v. REBECCA, born August 3, 1720.
- vi. E——, a son, born January 16, 1726.

1. SEABRED TAYLOR, son of Thomas and Elizabeth Taylor, was born in Watertown, March 11, 1642-3. In his childhood his parents removed to Reading. He was a soldier in King Philip's War. He was one of the soldiers in the garrison at Groton, 1675, and he served in the companies commanded by Capt. Samuel Mosely, Capt. Joseph Sill and Capt. Nathaniel Davenport, who was succeeded by Capt. Edward Tyng. In the admission of grantees of the Narraganset townships, which

Thirty Dunstable Families. 79

were granted to the soldiers of King Philip's War or to the heirs of those deceased, the right of Seabred Taylor, deceased, was granted to his son, Thomas, who became a grantee of Westminster, Mass.

Seabred Taylor married November 21, 1671, Mary Harrington, daughter of Richard and Elizabeth Harrington of Charlestown. About 1685, he lived a short time in Charlestown, but soon returned to Reading, where he died in 1714. His widow, Mary, died May 13, 1733. They had seven or more children.

- i. ELIZABETH, born March 6, 1674-5; married in Woburn, December 3, 1702, Thomas Grover of Reading.
- ii. MARY, born September 26, 1676; died young.
- iii. MARY, born July 9, 1678; married in Woburn, January 8, 1695-6, Dr. Thomas Stimpson of Reading, son of Dr. James Stimpson. Two of their sons were physicians.
- iv. JOHN, born January 16, 1681-2.
- v. JAMES, born June 20, 1688.
- vi. THOMAS, born May 21, 1692; married in Reading, December 20, 1722, Mary Goodwin. He removed to Sudbury, where five children were born and where his wife died June 16, 1735. He was a grantee of Westminster, Mass., and sold the same August 16, 1735, to Samuel Trumbull of Charlestown, Mass.
- 2. vii. EBENEZER, was older than Thomas and probably older than James. His birth is not recorded.

2. Dr. EBENEZER TAYLOR, son of Seabred and Mary (Harrington) Taylor, was born in Reading or Charlestown, Mass., about 1685. In a deed dated March 7, 1710, Seabred Taylor of Reading conveys certain tracts of land to Ebenezer Taylor "in consideration of love and affection I have and do bear unto my dutiful son, Ebenezer, and in further consideration of £7, that my said son hath paid unto my son in law Thomas Grover and £, 8. that he hath paid unto my son in law Stimson."

He studied medicine with Dr. Thomas Stimson, and removed to Dunstable before 1711. He was the first resident physician here and he remained in practice many years. In 1724 and 1725, Dr. Ebenezer Taylor was paid for medicine and medical attendance on Joseph Chamberlain, a soldier, and Jabez Davis, a sick soldier. From 1711 to 1720, Ebenezer Taylor of Dunstable bought and sold many parcels of land in Dunstable and in Medford, Mass. In the conveyances he is styled a bricklayer, a mason and a husbandman, and in no instance is he called a physician. His wife named in the deeds was Mary, but a record of his marriage or of his death has not been discovered.

Dr. Samuel Colburn, an aged man of Dracut, married in 1755, Mary Taylor of Dunstable. It is probable that she was the widow of Dr. Ebenezer Taylor. Of the children of Dr. Ebenezer and Mary Taylor, a record of two sons follows.

2. BENJAMIN TAYLOR, son of Dr. Ebenezer, was born in 1733. He lived in Dunstable. Of good ability and superior education he occupied a foremost position among his townsmen. He was a soldier in the Revolution. He married Martha Lyon of Merrimack. They had seven or eight children. There is record of the birth of seven, and Secomb's Amherst says there were two daughters, one of whom married a Woods and one a Merrill. Gravestones in the Old Cemetery inform that "Mr. Benjamin Taylor son of Dr. Ebenezer Taylor died November 17, 1787 in the 55th year of his age." "Mrs. Martha Taylor, wife of Mr. Benja' Taylor died June 16, 1817 in the 79th year of her age."

  i. DAVID, born February 6, 1757. He was a soldier in Capt. Butterfield's company, Lexington alarm, 1775, and subsequently enlisted again and died in the service, probably in 1776.

  ii. BENJAMIN, born March 8, 1759. He served three years, 1777-1780, in Col. Cilley's regiment . He married in Ipswich, August 6, 1782, Anna Lowe, born 1761, daughter of Joshua and Anna Lowe. He was a soldier in the Revolution and also a seaman in the privatier service. About 1790, he removed to Maine. Two children were born in Dunstable. 1. *Cyrus Baldwin*, born May 8, 1783; 2. *Thomas*, born April 10, 1785.

  iii. EBENEZER, born September 11, 1761. He lived in Amherst, where he was a selectman and town officer many years. He married January 27, 1791, Lucy Weston, born February 27, 1773, daughter of Ebenezer and Lucy (Richardson) Weston of Amherst. He died August 10, 1835; she died July 24, 1834. For record of eleven children see History of Amherst.

  iv. ELEAZER, born December 11, 1763.

  v. BERTHIAH, born October 25, 1766; married November 26, 1787, Benjamin Woods, born in Dunstable, May 4, 1767, son of Oliver and Sarah Woods. Three children were born in Dunstable.

  vi. LUTHER, born April 21, 1769; married December 18, 1817, Esther Lovewell, born May 16, 1780, daughter of Gen. Noah Lovewell, see. He lived in Dunstable (Nashua)

Thirty Dunstable Families. 81

where he died August 29, 1843. His widow died May 12, 1859.

vii. MARTHA. There is no record of her birth; she married in Dunstable, May 28, 1789, David Merrill.

viii. ABNER, born April 20, 1779, removed to Maine.

3. JAMES TAYLOR, probably a son of Dr. Ebenezer Taylor, married in Hollis, April 21, 1768, Lois Butterfield of Dunstable. He lived in Hollis until 1772, when he removed to Merrimack. He was one of the volunteers of Lieut. Benjamin Bowers company 1777, and in 1778 he was quartermaster of Col. Stephen Peabody's regiment at Rhode Island. Three children were born in Hollis and three in Merrimack.

i. JAMES, born April 26, 1769.

ii. LOIS, born June 4, 1770.

iii. MOLLY, born January 21, 1772.

iv. SUSANNAH, born July 3, 1773.

v. EBENEZER, born March 31, 1775; died September 10, 1776.

vi. OLIVE, born January 21, 1777.

1. CHRISTOPHER TEMPLE, born about 1660, probably a son of Richard and Joanna Temple of Concord, Massachusetts. He came to Dunstable soon after 1680, and here married December 3, 1685, Alice Hassell, youngest daughter of Richard and Joan Hassell. See Hassell family. He was a constable in 1691 and was killed by the Indians September 28 of the same year. His widow, Alice, married second, January 10, 1694, Jacob Kendall, born January 25, 1661, son of Francis Kendall of Woburn. This was the second marriage of Jacob Kendall, and of this union there were eleven children born in Woburn. Of Christopher and Alice (Hassell) Temple there were three children.

i. JEREMIAH, born Dunstable, October 6, 1686.

ii. ALICE, born Dunstable, October 3, 1690; married Jacob Kendall, born in Woburn, January 12, 1686, son of Jacob and Persis (Hayward) Kendall. They lived in Woburn, Billerica, and after 1717, in Litchfield, where he was a selectman. He died 1742. Their children were *Christopher, Amos, Daniel, Alice, Persis, Elizabeth.*

iii. CHRISTOPHER, born Dunstable, October 3, 1690. He lived in Dunstable several years. After 1728, he lived in Merrimack and owned a farm and ferry next north of the Matthew Thornton farm at Thornton's ferry. About 1760 he sold the farm to James Matthews and removed to Littleton, Massachusetts. During the years of the union of Litchfield and Merrimack, he was a selectman, 1734, 1735, 1738, 1739 and 1741. He married in Andover, Mass., December 13, 1743, Jemima (Russell) Hunt, born 1704, daughter of Thomas and Phebe (Johnson) Russell and widow of Joseph Hunt. He died in Littleton, May 8, 1782. His widow died 1790. Their daughter, Jemima Temple, married May 21, 1768, Israel Read, born June 16, 1747, son of Israel and Hannah (Wyman) Read. She died in Littleton, November 18, 1783. He married, second, Mary Davis, and removed to Walpole, N. H.

1. EDWARD TYNG, came to America with his brother, William, about 1639. He was a brewer and a merchant of Boston, and for many years one of the most active and prominent men of his time. He was repeatedly honored by appointment to office in civil and military affairs. In 1660, he purchased of James Parker of Chelmsford, three thousand acres of land in the part of original Dunstable now Tyngsborough. Here his son Jonathan subsequently resided. Fox states that he removed to Dunstable in 1679, and that he died here December 28, 1681. He was buried on his estate at Tyngsborough. His grave is covered with a granite slab bearing an inscription which gives a different date of death. "Here lyeth the body of Mr. Edward Tyng, Esq. aged 71 years. Died December 17, Day 1681." It is generally accredited that the town was named for Dunstable, England, the early home of Mary, the wife of Hon. Edward Tyng.

Ten children of Edward and Mary Tyng born in Boston.

   i. HANNAH, born March 7, 1640; married May 8, 1661, Habijah Savage, born August 1, 1638, son of Thomas and Faith (Hutchinson) Savage. Harvard University 1659; merchant, Boston. Their daughter, Mary, was the second wife of Rev. Thomas Weld of Dunstable. Habijah Savage died 1669; she married, second, Daniel Gookin of Cambridge. She died in October, 1689.

   ii. MARY, born April 17, 1641.

2. iii. JONATHAN, born December 15, 1642.

   iv. DELIVERANCE, born August 6, 1645; married Daniel Searles. Lived in Boston several years. He was appointed governor of Barbadoes, and both died on the island. See Searles family.

   v. REBECCA, born March 23, 1647; died March 16, 1648-9.

3. vi. EDWARD, born 1649; baptized April 1, 1649.

   vii. REBECCA, born July 13, 1651; married 1668, Joseph Dudley, born in Roxbury, July 23, 1647, son of Governor Thomas

Thirty Dunstable Families. 83

Dudley. Harvard University, 1665. He was governor of Massachusetts succeeding Governor Simon Bradstreet. Subsequently councillor and chief justice of New York, deputy governor of the Isle of Wight and again governor of Massachusetts. He died April 2, 1720. She died September 21, 1722. They had twelve children. Of these *Rebecca* was the wife of Chief Justice Samuel Sewell; *Paul* was attorney general and chief justice; *Mary* married Francis Wainwright, married, second, April 7, 1730, Joseph Atkins of Newbury, where she died November 19, 1774. Her grandson, Dudley Atkins, born September 3, 1760, assumed the name of Dudley Atkins Tyng. He was the reporter of the supreme court; he edited seventeen volumes of the Massachusetts Law Reports. His son, Rev. Stephen Higginson Tyng, D. D., born March 1, 1800, was the eloquent and scholarly clergyman of the Episcopal church. Dudley Atkins Tyng inherited the Tyng estate in Tyngsboro.

viii. WILLIAM, born March 3, 1652-3.

ix. EUNICE, born March 8, 1655-6; married 1679, Rev. Samuel Willard, born at Concord, January 31, 1639-40, son of Major Simon Willard. He was pastor of the Old South Church and president of Harvard University. It was his second marriage. He died September 12, 1707. She died at Boston, January 14, 1720.

x. JOSEPH, born July 12, 1657; died July 30, 1658.

2. HON. JONATHAN TYNG, son of Hon. Edward, born December 15, 1642. He was one of the earliest settlers of the original township, and occupied a commanding position in civil and military affairs. He was colonel of the north or upper Middlesex regiment and was vested with unusual authority by the government of the province. In the successive wars with the Indians he was in command over a considerable territory and at all times secured the confidence of the government.

In 1676 he was appointed superintendent over the friendly Indians colonized at Dunstable. In this mission, Robert Parris was his deputy or assistant.

In the commission of King James II. to Governor Joseph Dudley, 1686, he is named one of the councillors. The same council was continued through the administration of Governor Andros. Crowning the honors of of a serviceable career he was a judge of the court of Middlesex county from 1702 to 1719.

In the superior qualities of his mind and character in the activities of his useful life and in the achievements of his descendants is found the inviting and substantial material for a volume of local history.

Hon. Jonathan Tyng married Sarah Usher, daughter of Hezekiah and Frances Usher of Boston. A record of her death has not been discovered. She was the mother of his children. He married, second, in Boston, May 30, 1706, Sarah (Gibbons-Richards) Davie. She was a daughter of William Gibbons, born in Hartford, August 17, 1645. She married James Richards of Hartford, who died July 29, 1680; she married, second, Humphrey Davie of Boston, his second wife. She died at Woburn, February 28, 1712-3 "in the 69 year of her age." Gravestone at Woburn. In Massachusetts Historical collections, sixth series, Vol II., page 298, is found an item by Samuel Sewall: "March 4 1713-14 went to Woburn to attend the funeral of Aunt Tyng being his second wife."

He married, third, Judith (Reyner) Fox, a daughter of Rev. John Reyner of Plymouth, Mass., and Dover, N. H., and widow of Rev. Jabez Fox of Woburn.

He removed from Dunstable to Woburn 1712 or 1713, and there died January 19, 1723-4. His widow died June 5, 1736, aged 98 years. Gravestones at Woburn.

Five children were born in Boston and seven in Dunstable.

 i.   FRANCIS, born December 11. 1669.
 ii.   ELIZABETH, born December 28, 1670.
 iii.   JONATHAN, born January 29, 1671-2; died young.
 iv.   JOHN, born September 1. 1673. Harvard University, 1691. Soon after his graduation he went to London, England, and there died in 1710. The statement that he was an officer in Queen Anne's War is erroneous.
 v.   MARY, born January 16, 1676-7.
4. vi.   WILLIAM, born April 22, 1679.
 vii.   HEZEKIAH, born May 29, 1680; died young.
 viii.   EDWARD, born March 2, 1681-2; died August 25, 1682.
 ix.   JOSEPH, born June 30, 1683; died young.
 x   JONATHAN, born September 29, 1686.
5. xi.   ELEAZER, born April 30, 1690.
 xii.   BARSHEBA, born February 5, 1694.

3.   HON. EDWARD TYNG, son of Edward and Mary Tyng, born in Boston, 1649; baptized April 1, 1649. He removed to Falmouth, 1680, and was commandant of the fort 1680 and 1681. He was commissioned a colonel. In 1686 he was named a councillor in the commission

of Governor Joseph Dudley, and was continued in that office through the administration of Governor Andros. Later he was appointed governor of Annapolis, and on the voyage thither he was captured by the French. He died, a prisoner, in France. He married at Falmouth, Elizabeth Clark, a daughter of Thaddeus and Elizabeth (Milton) Clark. They had four or more children.

   i. EDWARD, born 1683; died in Boston, September 8, 1755. He served in the navy with distinction. He was a commodore and senior officer at Louisbourg, 1745. He married at Boston, January 7, 1731, Ann Waldo, born April 13, 1708, daughter of Daniel and Hannah (Mason) Waldo of Boston. They had seven children: *Ann*, born October 22, 1733, married October 3, 1756, Thomas Smelt, of the British army; *Edward*, born January 19, 1734-5, an officer of the British army, died in England about 1776; *Jonathan*, born August 5, 1736, died young; *William*, born August 17, 1737, married Elizabeth Ross, daughter of Alexander and Elizabeth (Duguid) Ross of Falmouth. He was a merchant on Cornhill, Boston, several years. In 1767, he was appointed sheriff of Cumberland County, Maine, and removed to Falmouth. He was a representative 1772 and 1773. In the Revolution he was a royalist, and went to Halifax, Nova Scotia, and his property was confiscated. He was chief justice of the courts of Nova Scotia. In 1793, he returned to Maine and subsequently lived at Gorham, where he died, sine prole, December 10, 1807. *Hannah*, born October 25, 1738; *Mary*, born October 5, 1741.

  ii. JONATHAN, died young.

 iii. MARY, married Rev. John Fox, born May 10, 1678, son of Rev. Jabez Fox; the father and son were ministers at Woburn. He died December 12, 1756; she died in February, 1764. Seven children.

 iv. ELIZABETH, born about 1685; married, Boston, May 16, 1705, Samuel Franklin, born May 16, 1681, son of Josiah and Ann (Child) Franklin and half-brother of Benjamin Franklin.

4. MAJOR WILLIAM TYNG, son of Hon. Jonathan and Sarah (Usher) Tyng, was born at Dunstable, April 22, 1679. He was a soldier. At the outbreak of Queen Anne's War he was a lieutenant in command of a garrison in Dunstable. For the first time the Indians began to be active and troublesome in the winter season. By concurrent action of Massachusetts and New Hampshire, several companies were supplied with snowshoes and ordered out in the winter. These were called snowshoe men and the first company engaged in this service was organized at Dunstable and commanded by Capt.

William Tyng. This was the first company of snowshoe men. They were in the field thirty days and returned with five scalps for which the company received a bounty of two hundred pounds. The roll of the company is not preserved, but the dates and duration of service is stated in Massachusetts Council Records, Vol. IV., page 20: "A Muster Roll of the Foot Company under command of Capt. Wm Tyng containing account of wages for services from Dec. 28 to Jany 25 1703-4, four weeks £71-11^s including 25^s to Jonathan Prescott Junr Clyrurgion for looking after one of the men that came home sick."

He remained in the service from time to time until his death. Meanwhile he removed to Chelmsford and represented that town in the General Court. He was promoted to major, and in the summer of 1710, while in command of a battalion between Groton and Lancaster, he was severely wounded and was carried to Concord for medical attendance. He died in Concord, August 16, 1710. Several writers erroneously have credited a part or the whole of this military service to his brother John.

Major William Tyng married September 19, 1700, Lucy Clark, daughter of Rev. Thomas Clark of Chelmsford. She died April 25, 1708.

Three children of Major William and Lucy (Clark) Tyng.

i. SARAH, born March 11, 1702-3; married in Dunstable, September 12, 1728, Rev. Thomas Smith, born Falmouth, Maine, March 10, 1702, son of Thomas and Mary (Corwin) Smith. Harvard University, 1720. He was the first pastor of the First Church of Portland, and author of Smith's Historical Journal. She died October 1, 1742. Subsequently he was twice married. His first wife was the mother of his eight children. He died May 25, 1795. Their daughter, *Lucy*, married Thomas Sanders of Gloucester, Massachusetts. Of this marriage, one daughter, Lucy, married Paul Dudley Sargent, a colonel of the Revolution, who died in Sullivan, Maine. Another daughter, *Mary*, was the grandmother of the actress, Charlotte Sanders Cushman.

ii. JOHN, born January 28, 1705. Harvard University, 1725. He lived in Tyngsborough. He was a representative ten years, and a judge and chief justice of the Court of Common Pleas from 1763 to 1786. He was an amiable, useful man, and in an eminent degree he was respected and beloved by his fellow men. He died April 18, 1797. He married in Boston, August 29, 1732, Mary Morse, born in Boston, September 29, 1705, daughter of Benjamin and

Frances (Cook) Morse. She died October 15, 1783. Their daughter, *Elizabeth*, died August 6, 1782, aged 39 years. Their daughter, *Mary*, married June 3, 1779, Hon. John Pitts of Boston.

iii. MARY, born October 25, 1706; married at Woburn, October 7, 1723, Rev. Nathaniel Prentice, born 1698, son of Henry and Mary (Gove) Prentice of Cambridge. Harvard University, 1715. He was ordained over the church of Dunstable, 1720, and here died February 25, 1736-7. Gravestone. Five children of Rev. Nathaniel and Mary (Tyng) Prentice: *Mary*, born January 2, 1724-5; *William Henry*, born December 2, 1726; *Nathaniel*, born May 29, 1729; *Lucy; John*. Of these, Nathaniel died in England about 1769, William Henry married in Boston, April 12, 1753, Sarah Edes, born in Boston, April 17, 1729, daughter of Edward and Sarah (Mills) Edes. He was an engineer. He died in Littleton, Mass., April 12, 1798. Nathaniel Prentice, his son, was the clothier of New Ipswich.

5. COL. ELEAZER TYNG, son of Hon. Jonathan and Sarah (Usher) Tyng, was born in Dunstable, April 30, 1690. Harvard University, 1712. Through life he was an active, useful citizen. He was a colonel of the militia and a magistrate and was elected to many town and state offices. He inherited and improved the Tyng estate.

He married in Boston, July 24, 1716, Sarah Alford, born in Boston, March 17, 1693-4, daughter of Benjamin and Mary, and a sister of Hon. John Alford, who founded the Alford Prof. Natural Theology in Harvard University. She died May 23, 1753. He died May 21, 1782. Five children.

i. JONATHAN, born September 10, 1717; died young.

ii. SARAH, born April 22, 1720; married in Chelmsford, September 4, 1760, John Winslow, born, Boston, April 14, 1700, son of Edward and Hannah Winslow. He died November 3, 1788; she died October 29, 1791.

iii. BENJAMIN, born January 26, 1722, not married. He "died on a voyage to the Carolinas."

iv. JOHN ALFORD, born August 29, 1729, died September 4, 1775. He was not married.

v. JAMES, born March 6, 1731; married June 11, 1772, Rebecca Russell, born in Charlestown, February 27, 1746-7, daughter of Hon. James and Katherine (Greaves) Russell. He lived in Tyngsborough, where he died September 11, 1775. His widow, Rebecca, married, second, in Boston, January 27, 1778; John Lowell, Esq.

USHER. The most potent men in forwarding the settlement of Dunstable were Hon. Hezekiah Usher of Boston, Hon. Edward Tyng of Boston, Hon. Jonathan Tyng of Dunstable, a son of Hon. Edward and Dea. John Blanchard, whose name and the names of his sons and grandsons are firmly written in the annals of the town. The wife of Hon. Jonathan Tyng was Sarah, a daughter of Hezekiah Usher. Robert Usher, Jr., married a daughter of Dea. John Blanchard.

1. ROBERT USHER, a brother of Hon. Hezekiah, settled in Stamford, Connecticut. He was a representative and ever prominent in civil affairs. He married May 13, 1659, Elizabeth Jagger, widow of Jeremy Jagger. He died about 1670, leaving four children to the care of their uncle, Hon. Hezekiah Usher.

    i. ELIZABETH, born February 25, 1659; married August 2, 1680, John Solendine. See New England Register, 1906. Fox writes the name Lollendine.
2.   ii. ROBERT, born about 1662.
    iii. MEHITABLE.
    iv. SARAH.

2. ROBERT USHER, son of Robert and Elizabeth, was born in Stamford about 1662. He came to Dunstable in early life and here married January 23, 1694, Sarah Blanchard, a daughter of Dea. John Blanchard. See Blanchard family. Possibly they had more children, but mention of only two appears.

3.   i. JOHN, born May 31, 1696.
    ii. ROBERT, born June, 1700. He was a soldier under Capt. John Lovewell and was killed at Pigwacket, May 8, 1725.

3. JOHN USHER, son of Robert and Sarah (Blanchard) Usher, born May 31, 1696; married his cousin, Hannah Blanchard, daughter of Capt. Joseph and Abiah (Hassell) Blanchard. He lived in Dunstable and in Merrimack. He was a selectman and in the records of his time he receives frequent and honorable mention. An imperfect record of nine children has been collected from many sources.

    i. JOHN, born May 2, 1728; died young.
4.   ii. ROBERT, born April 9, 1730.
    iii. RACHEL, born 1732.

Thirty Dunstable Families. 89

- iv. HABIJAH, born August 8, 1734; died young.
- v. WILLIAM, born 1737; unmarried, died Hallowell, Maine.
- vi. JOHN, born December 5, 1741; died young.
- vii. ELIZABETH, born March 14, 1744; married at Amherst, February 27, 1773, Dea. James Robinson of Bow, New Hampshire. Their children were *James, William, Sarah, Elizabeth, Calvin, Harvey.*
- viii. ELEAZER, born June 16, 1746. He lived in Merrimack and Amherst. He married December 4, 1777, Widow Prudence Wilson, who died January 10, 1828. He died July 8, 1811. Four children: *Jacob,* born November 17, 1778; *William,* born March 25, 1780; *Patty,* born 1783; *Simeon,* born June 10, 1785, died April 28, 1786.
- ix. OLIVE, born August 27, 1749; died young.

4. ROBERT USHER, son of John, born in Merrimack, April 9, 1730, married 1754, Sarah Stearns, born in Merrimack, August 9, 1734, daughter of Zachariah and Sarah Stearns. They lived in Merrimack until 1790, when they removed to Medford, Mass., where he died of fever, October 13, 1793. His widow, Sarah, died March 25, 1794. Nine children.

- i. SARAH, born July 6, 1755; married John Nash.
- ii. ABIJAH, born February 15, 1757. No record found of his first marriage; his wife died at Medford, October 19, 1791. He married, second, December 20, 1795, Rebecca Kidder, born, Medford, September 11, 1772, daughter of Samuel Kidder.
- iii. HANNAH, born February 7, 1759; married John Peters.
- iv. ROBERT, born March 7, 1761; married in Nelson, N. H., October 19, 1784, Lydia Scollay, born in Harvard, December 13, 1768, daughter of Grover and Lois (Atherton) Scollay. Lived in Merrimack, N. H.
- v. DANIEL, born May 4, 1763; married in Framingham, December, 26, 1785, Lois Park, daughter of Gideon and Hannah (Fuller) Park. He married, second, in Danvers, October, 1795, Margaret Carroll, born March 25, 1768, daughter of Patrick and Amy Carroll. He died in Danvers, May 17, 1848.
- vi. FANNY, born 1764; married December 23, 1798, Daniel Wyer. He died at Medford, June 14, 1817.
- vii. JOHN, born 1766.
- viii. MARY, born 1768; married November 23, 1800, Wyman Weston.
- ix. ELEAZER, born November 23, 1770. He married October 6, 1799, Fanny Bucknam. Lived in Medford. He died April 9, 1852. His wife died December 28, 1848. The

youngest of their eleven children was Roland G. Usher, born January 6, 1823. He was paymaster, U. S. A., 1861-1865; mayor of Lynn 1866, and warden of state prison 1883-1886.

1. DEA. CORNELIUS WALDO was born in England about 1624. He settled in Ipswich and there married Hannah Cogswell, a daughter of John and Elizabeth (Thompson) Cogswell. He sold his house and lot in Ipswich in 1654, and soon removed to Chelmsford. He was active and prosperous, owning large parcels of land. The story of the Waldo farm in Dunstable is well known. This led to a residence here of his sons John, Cornelius and Daniel, but none of these remained many years. While they were in Dunstable they were prominent in the affairs of the settlement. Dea. Waldo died in Chelmsford, January 3, 1700. Three of his ten children were residents a few years in Dunstable.

  i. JOHN, born in Ipswich; married Rebecca Adams, daughter of Samuel and Rebecca (Graves) Adams of Chelmsford. He lived in Dunstable from about 1678 to 1688. He was a soldier in King Philip's War. He was in Capt. Wheeler's company which met the Indians at a disadvantage near Brookfield in August, 1675. In the encounter, eight of Capt. Wheeler's company were killed and five were wounded. "The fifth was John Waldo of Chelmsford, who was not so dangerously wounded as the rest." He was a representative, 1689. He removed to Windham, Connecticut. He died before 1702. His children were: *John*, born May 19, 1678; *Catherine*, born 1680; *Edward*, born April 23, 1684; *Rebecca*, born August 6, 1686; *Ruth;* *Sarah*, baptized, Boston, December 6, 1691, married July 4, 1715, Jehosaphat Holmes; *Abigail.*

  ii. CORNELIUS, born about 1655. He served in King Philip's War, and subsequently lived a few years in Dunstable, but soon removed to Boston. He married Faith Peck, born in Boston, December 8, 1658, daughter of Thomas and Elizabeth Peck. He probably died before 1700. Four children: *Cornelius*, born November 17, 1684; *Elizabeth*, born January 7, 1686-7; *Rachel*, born April 20, 1690; *Judith*, born January 25, 1691-2.

  iii. DANIEL, born August 16, 1657; married Susannah Adams, a sister of the wife of his brother John. After a residence in Dunstable of a few years, he removed with his brother John, to Connecticut. His children were: *Susannah*, born 1684; *Hannah*, born July 17, 1687; *Bethia*, born August 20, 1688; Daniel, born March 25, 1692; Rebecca, born February 5, 1693-4; *Marah*, born February 10, 1695-6; *Esther*, born January 3, 1698; *Zachariah*, born November 25, 1701.

Thirty Dunstable Families. 91

1. SAMUEL WARNER was born in Ipswich, 1640. His father, John Warner, removed from Ipswich to Brookfield, 1665, and was one of the three who secured the Indian deed of the township. At the destruction of Brookfield, 1675, John Warner and several of his sons retired to Hadley and subsequently resided in that town or immediate vicinity.

    Samuel Warner participated with his father and his brothers in the founding of Brookfield and in 1673 was one of the petitioners for the incorporation of the town, but there is no evidence that he removed his family from Ipswich until he removed to Dunstable very soon after 1680. He was one of the proprietors and was one of the seven male members of the church of Dunstable at its organization, December 16, 1685. He died about 1703.

    He married at Ipswich, October 21, 1662, Mercy Swan, born July 4, 1640, daughter of Richard Swan of Rowley. She died at Dunstable, April 3, 1683. He married, second, May 4, 1685, Mary (Martin) Swallow, widow of Ambrose Swallow of Chelmsford, see.

    Six children of the first wife born in Ipswich, and one of the second wife born in Dunstable.

    i. PRISCILLA. born September 25, 1666; married December 19, 1688, Thomas Cummings, born October 6, 1658, son of John and Sarah (Howlet) Cummings.
    ii. SAMUEL, born July 5, 1668, removed to Connecticut.
    iii. JOHN, born August 2, 1670; died July 14, 1671.
    iv. DOROTHY, born June 2, 1672.
    v. SARAH, born May 28, 1674.
    vi. RICHARD, born August 13, 1676. He lived in Groton. He married May 7, 1709, Sarah Gilson, widow of John Gilson. They had four children born in Groton.
    vii. ELEAZER, born January 27, 1686-7. He lived a few years in Brookfield, removing to New Braintree, where he died February 28, 1776. In the Indian wars of his time he served as a private, corporal, sergeant, lieutenant and captain, and was moderator, assessor and selectman of New Braintree. He married December 4, 1722, Prudence Barnes, daughter of Thomas Barnes who died February 25, 1770. Of their ten children, seven sons served in the French and Indian War and three died in the service.

1. REV. THOMAS WELD, the first minister of Dunstable, was born in Roxbury, June 1, baptized June 12, 1653. He was a son of Thomas and Dorothy (Whiting) Weld, grandson of Rev. Thomas Weld, and maternal grandson of

Rev. Samuel Whiting of Lynn. He graduated at Harvard University 1671, and was admitted to the church of Roxbury, April 27, 1678. He studied divinity with Rev. Samuel Danforth and began preaching in Dunstable as early as 1679. The church was gathered and Mr. Weld was ordained December 16, 1685. The churches of Exeter, Hampton, Dover and Portsmouth are of earlier foundation. It was the fifth church organized within the limits of New Hampshire. At that date Dunstable was within the jurisdiction of Massachusetts. If the limit of these family registers would permit, much could be written in commendation of the first minister of Dunstable. It is probable that preaching was suspended two years or more during the Indian hostilities beginning in 1691, and he died at the beginning of Queen Anne's War, June 7, 1702. The inscription upon the monument, erected in 1876, that he "probably was massacred by the Indians" is not credited.

Rev. Thomas Weld married in Medford, November 9, 1681, Elizabeth Wilson, born 1656, a daughter of Rev. John and Sarah (Hooker) Wilson. Her father was the first minister of Medfield, her grandfather, Rev. John Wilson, was the first minister of Boston, and her maternal grandfather, Rev. Thomas Hooker, was the first minister of Hartford. She died at Dunstable, July 29, 1687. He married, second, at Cambridge, May 22, 1700, Mary Savage, born August 27, 1667, daughter of Hon. Habijah and Hannah (Tyng) Savage of Boston, and granddaughter of Hon. Edward Tyng. Hon. Jonathan Tyng of Dunstable, was her uncle. She died at the home of her son, Rev. Habijah Weld, in Attleborough, June 2, 1731. There were four children of the first and two of the second wife.

i. ELIZABETH, born October 13, 1682.

ii. THOMAS, born February 7, 1683-4. In the will of Rev. John Wilson of Medfield, dated August 20, 1691, several parcels of land are devised to "my beloved grandchild Thomas Weld." He graduated at Harvard University, 1701, and the following year he was a school teacher in Chelmsford. Capt. Bowers, Cornet Hill, and Eleazer Brown, the town committee "Agreed with Sir Weld to be our school master half a year for £15. y^e sd. Sir Weld begun to keep school on y^e 1$^{st.}$ of October, 1702."

He united with the church of Roxbury in 1704 and died the same year, as appears in the church records of 1704.

Thirty Dunstable Families. 93

"Thomas Weld, A. B. pius juvenis premature objit in Christo circiter viginti annos natus."

iii. ELEAZER, born January 5, 1684-5; died April 11, 1686.
iv. JOHN, born February 5, 1685-6; died July 25, 1686.
v. SAMUEL, born March 4, 1700-1701.
vi. HABIJAH SAVAGE, born July 2, 1702, posthumous. He was baptized at Cambridge, by Rev. William Brattle, August 9, 1702. He graduated at Harvard University, 1723, and was ordained at Attleborough, Mass., October 1, 1727. Here he preached with great acceptance fifty-five years. He died May 4, 1782. He married October 17, 1728, Mary Fox, born October 26, 1706, daughter of Rev. John and Mary (Tyng) Fox of Woburn. They had fifteen children.

1. SAMUEL WHITING, son of Rev. Samuel and Dorcas (Chester) Whiting of Billerica, grandson of Rev. Samuel and Elizabeth (St. John) Whiting of Lynn, was born in Billerica, January 19, 1662-3. He was one of the first settlers in Dunstable and the cause of his settlement here is easily discerned. In consideration of money advanced by John Whiting, an alderman of Boston in England, and a brother of Rev. Samuel Whiting of Lynn, the General Court granted him, October 16, 1660, four hundred acres in Dunstable, bounded by Salmon brook and the Merrimack river. The title immediately passed from John to his brother, Rev. Samuel, and from him to his grandson, Samuel.

Samuel Whiting was town clerk, selectman, and is frequently and honorably mentioned in the records. His home was one of the fortified garrisons. The record is not clear but at one time he was held in captivity by the Indians, and in 1713, the General Court, on account of wounds and sufferings, granted him ten pounds.

He married at Dunstable, January 27, 1686-7, Elizabeth Read, daughter of Christopher Read, see. He died at Billerica, March 8, 1715. His widow married, second, 1717, William Patten, born May 12, 1671, son of Thomas and Rebecca (Paine) Patten. He lived in Billerica. He died of smallpox at Cambridge, while attending the General Court. The children of Samuel and Elizabeth Whiting were:

2. i. SAMUEL, born October 22, 1687.
   ii. ELIZABETH, born April 26, 1689; married December 19, 1710, Rev. Samuel Ruggles, son of Samuel and Martha (Woodbridge) Ruggles of Roxbury. He was pastor at Billerica. She died July 29, 1727. Eight children.

- iii. CATHERINE, born June 10, 1691; married December 31, 1714, John Lane, born October 20, 1691, son of Col. John and Susannah (Whipple) Lane. They lived in Billerica, where she died April 1, 1731. Six children.
- iv. LEONARD, born August 12, 1693, probably settled in Connecticut.
- v. JOSEPH, born December 14, 1695; probably settled in Connecticut.
- vi. MARY, born January 1, 1701; married June 4, 1735, her cousin, Oliver Whiting, born March 29, 1691, son of Oliver and Anna (Danforth) Whiting of Billerica.
- vii. DORCAS, born 1703; married December 30, 1725, Rev. Benjamin Ruggles, a son of Samuel and Martha (Woodbridge) Ruggles. He was pastor of Middleboro, now Lakeville, where he was ordained November 17, 1725; dismissed in December, 1753.
- viii. JOHN, born March 11, 1706; died before 1718.

2. SAMUEL WHITING, son of Samuel, born October 22, 1687. He was a soldier in Lovewell's third expedition and was wounded May 8, 1725. He lived in Dunstable, and was living 1748. He was one of the supporters of Rev. Samuel Bird. I have found no record of his marriage or death. He had at least one son.

3. i. JOSEPH, born 1727.

3. JOSEPH WHITING, son of Samuel, was born 1727. He married June 11, 1761, Abigail Chamberlain, born February 27, 1743, daughter of Thomas and Susannah Chamberlain. He lived many years in Dunstable, where he was town clerk and often employed in town business. In 1793, he removed to the north part of Lyndeborough. He died in Merrimack, 1807. His wife, Abigail, died in Dunstable, April 19, 1779. Ten children were born in Dunstable.

- i. JOSEPH, born November 13, 1761; died April 21, 1778.
- ii. SAMUEL, born June 30, 1763; married March 31, 1795, Anstress Barker. He lived in Amherst where he died March 24, 1805. He was a merchant. Three, probably more, children. (1) *Samuel*, born 1797, Dartmouth College, 1818, was a lawyer in Mason, where he died September 24, 1829. He married July 3, 1827, Hannah Russell, daughter of Hubbard and Sarah (Warren) Russell of Mason. (2) *Anstress*, born 1803, died August 5, 1803. (3) *Mary*, born 1805, died April 23, 1805.
- iii. SUSANNAH, born March 20, 1765.
- iv. LEONARD, born January 16, 1767.

- v. OLIVER, born January 29, 1769; married May 2, 1793, Hannah Marshall, born in Billerica, October 24, 1774, daughter of Isaac and Abigail (Brown) Marshall. He lived in Lyndeborough. He died July 15, 1815; she died in October, 1843. Eight children. See History of Lyndeborough.
- vi. WILLIAM, born September 28, 1770. He married April 8, 1793, Mary Thompson, born October 21, 1773, daughter of Asa and Mary (Swallow) Thompson of Tyngsborough. He lived in Merrimack, where he died June 4, 1813. She died at Pepperell, July 1, 1839.
- vii. ELIZABETH, born July 16, 1772.
- viii. THOMAS, born October 20, 1774; died at Amherst, December 16, 1801.
- ix. ABIGAIL, born August 13, 1776.
- x. JONATHAN, born February 18, 1778; died at Amherst, December 17, 1802.

1. JAMES WHITING, a record of his birth and names of his parents have not been found. He married Hepsibah Foster, born March 12, 1696-7, daughter of Eli and Judith (Keyes) Foster of Chelmsford. He removed soon after his marriage to Chester, N. H., where he resided from 1725 to 1736. He was one of a committee to distribute the common land among the proprietors in 1725, and a constable in 1726. He removed to Dunstable 1736, and was included in Hollis, when that town was severed from Dunstable. He died in Hollis in 1774. The two youngest of his nine children were born in Dunstable.

- i. JONATHAN, born April 13, 1722.
- ii. JAMES, born June 23, 1724.
- iii. PHEBE, born in Chester, January 29, 1726.
- iv. THOMAS, born in Chester, January 29, 1728.
- v. MARY, born in Chester, June 2, 1730.
- vi. MICHAEL, born in Chester, March 29, 1734; removed to Guilford, Vermont.
- vii. DORCAS, born in Chester, April 5, 1736.
- viii. DAVID, born in Dunstable, September 13, 1738.
- ix. HEPSIBAH, born in Dunstable, 1740.

INDEX OF NAMES.

The registers are arranged in alphabetical order and persons mentioned as members of a family are not indexed. This index contains the names of persons connected by marriage and those incidentally mentioned.

Abbot, Mary, 61.
Adams, Elizabeth, 62.
  Pelatiah, 5.
  Rebecca, 90.
  Ruth, 5.
  Samuel, 90.
  Susannah, 90.
Alford, John, 87.
  Sarah, 87.
Ames, John, 63.
  Priscilla, 63.
  Stephen, 63.
Andrus, Desire, 24.
Archibald, David, 12, 13.
  Jane, 13.
  Martha, 13.
  Matthew, 13.
Aspinwall, William, 47.
Atherton, Lois, 89.
Atkins, Dudley, 83.
  Joseph, 83.
Atwater, Abigail, 25.
Ayers, Joseph, 41.

Bachelder, Seaborn, 17, 57.
  William, 17, 57.
Bailey, Sybel, 20, 77.
Baker, Henry M., 39.
  John, 47.
  Joseph, 27, 39.
  Thomas, 38.
Ball, Anna, 46.
Bancroft, Ebenezer, 17.
Barker, Anstress, 94.
  William, 10.
Barnard, Benjamin, 59.
Barnes, Prudence, 91.
  Thomas, 91.
Barrett, Anna, 68.
  John, 67.
  Mehitable, 25.
  Sarah, 67.
  Thomas, 25, 68.

Barron, Benjamin, 58.
  Ellis, 58.
  Ellis, 59.
  Moses, 66.
  Samuel, 55.
  William, 28.
Bartlett, Abigail, 46.
  Ebenezer, 46.
Batchelder, Joseph, 26.
  Mary, 26.
Bates, Hannah, 61.
Beale, Benjamin, 32.
  Bridget, 32.
  Martha, 15.
  Samuel, 35.
  William, 15, 35.
Bedel, Sarah, 43.
  Timothy, 28.
Behoney, see Honey
Bennett, Benjamin, 63.
  Joseph, 63.
  Mary, 15, 63.
  Moses, 5.
  Samuel, 48.
Bent, Elizabeth, 59.
  Hopestill, 59.
  Peter, 59.
Bird, Samuel, 40, 70, 94.
Bixby, Abigail, 65.
  David, 65.
  Thankful, 65.
Blanchard, Ann, 3.
  Augustus, 32, 40.
  Edward, 88.
  Elizabeth, 20, 61.
  Grace, 20.
  Hannah, 57, 61, 88.
  John, 17, 56, 57, 61, 88.
  Joseph, 29, 40, 41, 61, 88.
  Mary, 17.
  Rachel, 76.
  Sarah, 88.

Blanchard, Susannah, 43.
  Thomas, 61.
  William, 3.
Blodgett, Anna, 73.
  Bridget, 75.
  Jemima, 75.
  John, 5.
  Josiah, 75.
  Mary, 5.
  Thomas, 5.
Blood, Anna, 4.
  Elizabeth, 68.
  Hannah, 4, 68.
  Mary, 5.
  Nathaniel, 4, 68.
  Sybel, 72.
Borland, Francis, 50.
Boutelle, Lucy, 75.
Bowers, Benjamin, 81.
  Jesse, 45.
  William, 45.
Boynton, Ruth, 76.
Brackett, Alice, 4.
  Hannah, 4.
  Richard, 4.
Bradstreet, Bridget, 2.
  Elizabeth, 10.
  Humphrey, 2.
  Martha, 2.
  Simon, 83.
Brattle, William, 93.
Breed, Elizabeth, 57.
Brenton, William, 16.
Bridgeman, Henry, 34.
Briggs, Hannah, 57.
Brigham, Hepsibah, 43.
Brown, Abigail, 59, 95.
  Eleazer, 92.
  Elizabeth, 59.
  Hopestill, 59.
  James, 5.
  Mary, 59.
  Rebecca, 7.

Index.

Bucknam, Fanny, 89.
Bulkeley, Peter, 17.
Burge, Rebecca, 63.
Burlingame, John, 28.
Burnap, Elizabeth, 8.
  Martha, 75.
Burrage, John, 57.
  Thomas, 4, 57.
Burroughs, Betsey, 33.
  Joseph, 33.
Burton, Sarah, 52.
Butler, Elizabeth, 51.
Butterfield, Benjamin, 64.
  Betsey, 31.
  Ebenezer, 74.
  Lois, 81.
  Mary, 64.
  Rachel, 74.
  Rhoda, 31.
  Samuel, 74.
  Sarah, 64.
Buxton, Mary, 68.
  Stephen, 68.

Calef, Hannah, 10.
  Robert, 10.
  Sarah, 10.
Carleton, Jeremiah, 78.
  Joseph, 78.
Carlton, Rebecca, 55.
Carroll, Amy, 89.
  Margaret, 89.
  Patrick, 89.
Cash, James, 30.
Chamberlain, Abigail, 94.
  Jane, 61.
  John, 37.
  Joseph, 79.
  Susannah, 94.
  Thomas, 94.
Chapman, Mary, 71.
Cheney, John, 72.
Chester, Dorcas, 93.
Child, Ann, 85.
  Ruth, 46.
Chittenden, Beulah, 25.
  Mary, 24.
  Thomas, 24, 25.
Clark, Abraham, 78.
  Elizabeth, 85.
  Lucy, 86.
  Rebecca, 55.
  Rose, 3.
  Thaddeus, 85.
  Thomas, 86.
Clogston, John, 28.

Clogston, Mary, 28.
Codman, Rachel, 13.
Coggin, Sarah, 13.
Cogswell, Hannah, 90.
  John, 90.
Colburn, Hannah, 55.
  Samuel, 80.
Combs, Susannah, 2.
Converse, Abigail, 7.
  Jesse, 7.
  John, 7.
  Joseph, 7.
  Joshua, 7, 76.
  Rachel, 7, 76.
  Zebulon, 7.
Cook, Frances, 87.
Cooke, Andrew, 3, 35, 37.
  Mary, 37.
Cooper, William, 47.
Corey, John, 69.
  Mary, 69.
Corwin, Mary, 86.
Cotton, Sarah, 12.
Courser, William, 34.
Cowper, Jane, 17, 57.
Cox, Esther, 13.
Craze, Richard, 36.
Crispe, Benjamin, 57.
  Bridget, 57.
  Mary, 57.
Cromwell, John, 57.
Crosby, Esther, 13.
  Joel, 13.
  John, 13.
  Josiah, 13.
  Samson, 13.
Cumbey, Humphrey, 17.
  Robert, 17.
  Sarah, 17.
Cummings, Asenath, 73.
  Ebenezer, 78.
  Eleazer, 45.
  Elizabeth, 19, 26, 62, 78.
  Ephraim, 51.
  Isaac, 49.
  Israel W., 45.
  James, 20.
  Jeremiah, 20, 72.
  John, 4, 18, 19, 27, 62, 78, 91.
  Jonathan, 6.
  Josiah, 6, 77.
  Mary, 20, 62.
  Nathaniel, 19.
  Oliver, 20, 77.
  Priscilla, 6, 51, 54.

Cummings, Rachel, 62.
  Sarah, 18, 74, 78, 91.
  Simeon, 73.
  Thomas, 6, 91.
  William, 27.
Cushing, Samuel, 77.
Cushman, Charlotte Sanders, 86.
Cutler, Sarah, 53.
Cutter, Rebecca, 71.
Cutts, Samuel, 11.

Dane, Mary, 74.
Danforth, Abigail, 11.
  Anna, 94.
  David, 14.
  Elizabeth, 14.
  Jonathan, 16.
  Joseph, 53, 76.
  Josiah, 21.
  Lucy, 53.
  Mary, 76.
  Orpah, 54.
  Rhoda, 21.
  Samuel, 92.
  Timothy, 14.
  William, 54.
Darrell, Elizabeth, 58.
Davenport, Nathaniel, 47, 78.
Davie, Humphrey, 84.
  Sarah (Gibbons Richards), 84.
Davis, Elizabeth, 7.
Davis, Jabez, 79.
  Mary, 82.
Dean, Sarah, 8.
Derbyshire, John, 4.
Dinsmore, Samuel, 10.
Druse, Mary, 5.
Dudley, Joseph, 5, 82, 83, 85.
  Mary, 5.
  Thomas, 82.
Duguid, Elizabeth, 85.
Duncklee, Jacob, 53.
Dunster, Jason, 71.
  Rebecca, 71.
Dwight, Betsey, 74.

Eastman, Amos, 70.
  Jonathan F., 11.
  Joseph F., 11.
Eaton, Hannah, 10.
  Rebecca, 68.
Eddy, Mary Baker, 39.
Edes, Edward, 87.

Index.   99

Edes, Sarah, 87.
Elliot, Elizabeth, 12.
 William, 32.
Emerson, Amos, 28.
 Daniel, 70.
 Hannah, 70.
 Lucy, 70.
Erwin, Miriam, 63.
Ettridge, S. I., 55.

Farmer, Sarah, 27.
Farrar, Rebecca, 77.
 Timothy, 41.
Farwell, Henry, 6, 19, 36.
 Jonathan, 43.
 Joseph, 11.
 Josiah, 36, 38.
 Mary, 44.
 Oliver, 11, 44.
 Rachel, 43.
 Rebecca, 11.
 Susannah, 43.
Ferguson, Archibald, 2.
Fitch, Elizabeth, 7.
 Joseph, 7.
 Samuel, 7.
 Sarah, 13.
 Thaddeus, 7.
 Zerviah, 25.
Fisher, Jennet, 13.
Fiske, Abigail, 59.
 Nathan, 52.
Flanders, Hannah, 10.
Fletcher, Elizabeth, 75.
 Hannah, 77.
 Jonathan, 75.
 Joseph, 75.
 Robert, 8.
 Sarah, 61, 62.
 William, 17.
Folsom, David, 10.
 Dorothy, 10.
 William, 10.
Foot, Isaac, 28.
Fosdick, Martha, 50.
Foster, Eli, 95.
 Hepsibah, 95.
 Prudence, 6.
Fox, Jabez, 84, 85.
 John, 85, 93.
 Judith (Reyner), 84.
 Mary, 92.
Franklin, Benjamin, 85.
 Josiah, 85.
 Samuel, 85.
French, Benjamin, 14, 40, 77.

French, Frederick, 11.
 Josiah, 14.
 Theodore, 33.
 Thomas, 11.
Fuller, Hannah, 89.
 Sarah, 10.

Gay, Mary, 46.
Gibbons, William, 84.
Gilman, Peter, 28.
Gilson, John, 91.
 Jonathan, 52.
 Naomi, 53.
 Sarah, 91.
Glasford, Miranda, 28.
Goble, Abigail, 5.
Godding, Jonathan C., 47.
 Peter, 47.
 Spencer, 47.
Goffe, Hannah, 56.
Goffe, John, 28, 39, 57, 66.
Goldthwait, Elizabeth, 46.
Goodnow, Asenath, 46.
 Ephraim, 46.
Goodwin, Mary, 79.
Gookin, Daniel, 82.
Gould, Francis, 21.
 Hannah, 21.
 Johu, 21.
 Samuel, 21.
Gove, Lydia, 43.
 Mary, 87.
Gragg, Elizabeth, 63.
Grant, Francis, 2.
 John, 2.
 Susannah, 2.
Graves, Rebecca, 90.
 Sarah, 68.
Green, Hannah, 68.
 Mary, 69.
 Samuel, 71.
 William, 60.
Greene, William, 47.
Grover, Thomas, 79.

Hale, Betty, 50.
 John, 40.
 Joseph, 40.
 Sarah, 33.
 Thomas, 40.
Hall, Mary, 71.
 Nathan, 71.
Hallet, Solomon, 13.
Hardy, Enos, 55.
 Mary, 50, 53, 71.

Nehemiah, 54.
Harrington, Adino, 46.
 Elizabeth, 79.
 Lucy, 46.
 Mary, 79.
 Richard, 79.
Hart, John, 7.
 Mary, 2.
 Samuel, 2.
Hartwell, Samuel, 63.
 Sarah, 63, 72.
Harwood, Watson H., 28.
Haseltine, Betsey, 43.
 John, 43.
Hassell, Abiah, 6, 88.
 Alice, 81.
 Anna, 6-36.
 Benjamin, 37, 78.
 Esther, 27, 39, 59, 60.
 Joan, 81.
 Joseph, 36, 37.
 Richard, 59, 81.
Hastings, Esther, 46.
Haynes, Abigail, 59.
Hayward, Persis, 81.
Hazen, Benjamin, 5.
 Edward, 5.
 Jane, 5.
Heaton, Jabez 36.
Henchman, Thomas, 48.
Hill, Bathsheba, 14.
 Jonathan, 76.
 Lucy, 76.
 Mary, 76.
 Phebe Cole, 44.
Hilliard, Samuel, 44.
Hills, Elizabeth, 3, 61.
 Hannah, 57.
 Joseph, 3, 61.
Holden, Rachel, 50.
 Richard, 50.
 Sarah, 63.
 Stephen, 50.
Holmes, Jehosaphat, 90.
Honey, Bridget, 41.
 Caty, 21, 42.
 John, 21, 42.
 Peter, 3, 41.
Hooker, Sarah, 92.
 Thomas, 92.
House, Combs, 28.
 Susannah, 28.
Houstan, Rachel, 30.
Howlet, Sarah, 18, 91.
Hubbard, Abigail, 11, 44.
 Jonathan, 7.
 Rebecca, 7.

Index.

Hubbard, Sarah C., 44.
Hull, John, 17.
Humphries, Francis, 71.
Hunt, Hepsibah, 50.
  Jemima (Russell), 82.
  Jeremiah, 71.
  Joseph, 82.
  Mary, 71.
  William, 50, 71.
Huntington, Lydia, 24.
  Matthew, 24.
Hutchins, Jedediah, 29.
Hutchinson, Asa, 25.
  Faith, 82.
Hyde, Eleazer, 15.
  Hannah, 15.
  Mindwell, 15.

Ingersol, Sarah, 58.

Jackson, Elizabeth, 2.
  Nancy, 46.
  Ruth, 51.
  Thaddeus, 46.
Jagger, Elizabeth, 88.
Jefts, Hannah, 48.
Jewell, James, 50.
Jewett, Joanna, 51.
Johnson, Dorothy, 10.
  Edward, 16.
  Hannah, 37.
  John, 37.
  Phebe, 82.

Kendall, Abigail, 73.
  Cheever, 59.
  Elizabeth, 72.
  Francis, 81.
  Isaac, 72.
  Jacob, 29, 81,
  Mary, 50.
  Susanna, 73.
  Temple, 72.
Keyes, Judith, 95.
Kidder, Benjamin, 57.
  Frederick, 38.
  Hannah, 45.
  Rebecca, 89.
  Samuel, 89.
Kimball, Priscilla, 63.
King, George, 12.
Kinsley, Elizabeth, 4, 19, 27, 78.
  Hannah, 4.
  Samuel, 4.
Knapp, Elijah, 71.
  Huldah, 16.

Lakin, Miriam, 63.
  William, 63.
Lamb, Sarah, 46.
Lane, John, 94.
  Mary, 76.
  Susannah, 7.
Langdon, Samuel 9.
Larkin, Mary, 63.
Lawrence, Hannah, 50.
  Sarah, 71.
Leach, Elizabeth, 45.
Learned, Hannah, 47.
Leonard, Lydia, 24.
Lepingwell, Isabel, 5.
  Michael, 5.
  Tabitha 5.
Linkfield, Edward 57.
Lippincott, Jacob, 12.
Longley, Sarah, 70.
Lovejoy, Phebe, 14.
Loveland, Irene Lyman, 44.
Lovewell, Bridget, 13.
  Elizabeth, 2, 3, 32.
  Esther, 80.
  Hannah, 66.
  John, 2, 3, 14, 29, 30, 32, 50, 66, 67.
  Jonathan 21, 32, 33.
  Joseph, 14.
  Lucy, 9.
  Molly, 20, 77.
  Nehemiah, 7, 28.
  Noah, 80.
  Patience, 2.
  Phebe, 14.
  Zaccheus, 9, 29, 30.
Lowe, Anna, 89.
  Joshua, 80.
Lowell, John, 33, 34, 87.
  Percival, 34.
Lund, Ephraim, 52.
  Jesse, 52.
  Joanna, 53.
  Jonathan, 54.
  Margaret, 62.
  Priscilla, 54.
  Rachel, 42.
  Sarah, 63.
  Thomas, 62.
  William, 42.
Luther, Charity, 24.
Lutwyche, Edward Goldstone, 39, 41.
Lyon, Martha, 80.
  Matthew, 25.

Marble, Elizabeth, 26.

Marks, Mary, 56.
  Patrick, 55, 56.
Marshall, Hannah, 95.
  Isaac, 95.
Martin, Bridget, 74.
  Mary, 67.
  Sarah, 28.
Mason, Hannah, 85.
Matthews, James, 81.
McClench, Elizabeth, 31.
Mead, Larkin, G., 7.
Meigs, Elizabeth, 24, 25.
Melvin, Josiah, 10.
Merrill, David, 81.
Metcalf, Joseph, 63.
Mills, Jacob, 42.
  John, 28.
  Martha, 42.
  Sarah, 87.
Milton, Elizabeth, 85.
Minot, James, 8.
Moor, Mary, 7.
Morrill, Mary, 31.
Morse, Benjamin, 86.
  Deborah, 37, 41.
  John, 15.
  Martha Jane, 47.
  Mary, 86.
  Nathaniel, 15.
  Samuel, 37, 41.
Mosely, Samuel, 78.
Muzzey, Benjamim, 48.

Nash, John, 89.
Newell, Ezra, 71.
Nichols, Joseph, 10.
  Moses, 10, 28.
Noyes, Dorothy, 58.
  Peter, 5.
Nutting, Elizabeth, 5.
  Jemima, 75.
  Jonathan, 69.
  Mary, 69.
  Sarah, 69.
  Susannah, 33.

Ober, Elizabeth, 53.
Oldham, Mary, 15.
Ordway, Jonathan, 29.
Osgood, Abigail, 78.
  Anna, 14.

Page, Albert Gallatin, 74.
  Betsey, 74.
  Edmund, 74.
  Frank Dwight, 74.
  Ruth, 46.

Index. 101

Page, Sarah, 74.
Paige, John, 7.
　Nathaniel, 7.
　Susannah, 7.
Paine, Rebecca, 93.
Park, Gideon, 89.
　Lois, 89.
Parker, Benjamin, 69.
　Caty, 52.
　David, 69.
　Deliverance, 6.
　Hannah, 4, 68.
　Jacob, 17.
　James, 69, 82.
　John, 16, 17.
　Lydia, 6.
　Mary, 69.
　Nathaniel, 6.
　Ruth, 76.
　Thomas, 74.
　William, 76.
Parkhurst, Abigail, 19.
　Isaac, 52.
　Mary, 5.
　Sarah, 76.
Parris, Robert, 4, 83.
Patten, Mary, 17.
　Samuel, 41.
　Thomas, 93.
　William, 93.
Peabody, Stephen, 81.
Pearson, Joseph, 57.
Peck, Elizabeth, 90.
　Faith, 90.
　Thomas, 90.
Pellet, Mary.
　Sarah, 74.
　Thomas, 74.
Perham, Sarah, 64.
　Susannah, 62, 75.
Perkins, George Hamilton, 14.
　Roger Eliot, 14.
　Timothy, 14.
Perley, Sidney, 2.
Perry, Anna, 6, 29, 36, 37.
　Esther, 27
　Obadiah, 27, 29, 37.
　William, 29.
Peters, John, 89.
Phelps, Hannah, 55.
Phillips, Deborah, 45.
　Theophilus, 15.
Pierce, Francis, 37.
　Rachel, 51, 52, 54.
　Stephen, 51, 52.
　Thankful, 52.

Pike, Isaac, 53.
　Sarah, 39.
Piper, Mary, 26.
Pitts, John, 87.
Pollard, Cummings, 55.
　Frances, 63.
　Lucy, 54.
　Solomon, 26.
　Thomas, 27.
Porter, Abigail, 24.
Powers, Nathan, 31.
Prentice, Henry, 87.
　John, 6.
　Nathaniel, 87.
Presby, Timothy, 55.
Prescott, Jonathan 86.
Preston, Charles Albert, 77.
　John, 77.
　Lucy Bancroft, 77.
　Lydia, 33.
　Samuel, 77.
Proctor, Hannah, 34.
　Olive Fletcher 73.
　Rebecca P., 74.
Putnam, John Jay, 7.
Read, Christopher, 93.
　Elizabeth, 93.
　Israel, 82.
　John, 54.
　Silas, 55.
　Thomas, 4.
　James, 28.
Reeves, Samuel, 59.
Reyner, John, 84.
Reynolds, Daniel, 28.
Rice, Chloe, 46.
　Isaac, 46.
　Nelly, 46.
Richards, James, 84.
Richardson, Abigail, 75.
　Josiah, 57.
　John, 20.
　Lucy, 13.
　Mary, 13, 21, 53, 56, 76, 80.
　Susannah, 6, 36.
　Sybel, 20.
　Thomas, 75.
Robbins, Esther, 70.
　Jonathan, 38, 48.
Robinson, James, 89.
Roby, Thomas, 50.
　William, 53.
Rogers, James, 28.
　Robert, 8.
Ross, Alexander, 85.

Ross, Elizabeth, 85.
Rowell, Artemas, 71.
Ruggles, Benjamim, 94.
　Samuel, 93, 94.
Rushton, Alice, 18.
Russell, Hannah, 94.
　Hubbard, 94.
　James, 87.
　Rebecca, 87.

Sabins, Joseph, 47.
Sammons, Martha, 24.
Sanders, David, 28.
　Patty, 28.
　Thomas, 86.
Sanderson, Susannah, 70.
Sargent, Nathaniel, 51.
　Olive, 51.
　Paul Dudley, 86.
Savage, Habijah 82, 92.
　Mary, 92.
　Thomas, 82.
Sawtell, Mary, 5.
　Zachariah, 5
Sawtelle, Andrew, 74.
Sawyer, Abigail, 7.
Scollay, Grover, 89.
　Lydia, 89.
Searles, Daniel, 82.
Selman, John, 2.
Sewell, Samuel, 83, 84.
Shattuck, Hannah, 62.
　William, 48, 62.
Shedd, Rachel, 55.
Shepard, Benjamin, 52.
Shurtleff, Giles, 45.
　Jonathan, 45.
Sill, Joseph, 78.
Smelt, Thomas, 85.
Smith, Benjamin, 8, 39, 43, 51, 53, 66, 67.
　Elias, 8, 12.
　Elizabeth, 8.
　Joanna, 53.
　Thomas, 86.
Snow, Abigail, 28.
　Rebecca, 33.
Solendine, John, 48, 88.
Souther, Anne Stickney, 14.
Spalding, Andrew, 48, 70.
　Betty, 9.
　Ebenezer, 5.
　Edward, 49.
　Hannah, 70.
　Henry, 48.

Spalding, Ira, 70.
Joanna, 70.
Joseph, 9.
Lucy, 61.
Rachel, 71-74.
Spear, Margaret, 13.
Stark, John, 8.
Starr, Augustus, 9.
Edward, 9.
John, 9.
Ebenezer, 9, 11.
Hannah, 9.
Jonathan, 9.
Rebecca, 9.
Sarah, 9.
Stearns, Abigail, 15.
John, 13.
Sarah, 89.
Zachariah, 89.
Stickney, Thomas, 14.
Stiles, Jacob, 72.
Prudence, 72.
Sarah, 72.
Stimpson, James, 79.
Thomas, 79.
Stockwell, Charlotte, 46.
Emmons, 46.
Stone, Mindwell, 33.
Stower, Joanna, 57.
Sumner, Hannah, 57.
Swallow, Ambrose, 91.
Mary, 91, 95.
Swan, Ebenezer, 6.
Josiah, 6.
Mercy, 91.
Prudence, 6.
Richard, 91.
Sylvester, Elizabeth, 2, 3, 34.
Esther, 36.
John, 3.
Joseph, 36.
Richard, 34, 35, 36.
Symmes, Thomas, 38.
Symonds, Nathaniel, 12.

Taplin, Hepsibah, 44.
John, 43, 44.
Mansfield, 43, 44.
Polly, 44.
Sophia, 44.
Taylor, Abraham, 48.
David, 49.
Elizabeth, 30, 48, 62.
John, 30.
Mary, 72, 73, 74, 80.
Rufus, 14.
Samuel, 72.

Taylor, Susannah, 72.
Timothy, 7.
Temple, Christopher, 29, 37, 59.
Thompson, Asa, 95.
Elizabeth, 90.
Mary, 95.
Todd, James, 28.
Toothaker, Allin, 20, 77.
Esther (French) 76.
Torrey, Naomi, 34, 35.
Town, Peter, 60.
Towne, Sarah, 52.
Thomas, 52.
Townsend, Martin, 29, 60.
Treadwell, Elizabeth, 12.
Jacob, 12.
Samuel, 12.
Trowbridge, Caleb, 74.
Hannah, 14.
Trumbull, Samuel, 79.
Twiss, Betsey, 71.
Tyng, Deliverance, 64.
Dudley Atkins, 83.
Edward, 64, 78, 88, 92.
Eleazer, 7, 49.
Hannah, 92.
Jonathan, 56, 64, 88, 92.
Mary, 93.
Stephen Higginson, 83.
William, 4, 37.

Underwood, Elizabeth, 75.
Hannah, 63.
James, 50.
Remembrance, 57.
Upton, Abigail, 68.
Dorcas, 68.
Joseph, 68.
Mehitable, 68.
Usher, Frances, 84.
Hezekiah, 84.
Robert, 4.
Sarah, 84, 85, 87.

Varnum, Jean, 51.
Joseph, 60.
Thomas, 51.

Waddell, John, 13.
Wadkins, John, 15.
Wadsworth, Samuel, 66.
Wainwright, Francis, 83.

Waldo, Ann, 85.
Daniel, 85.
John, 90.
Walker, Elizabeth, 7.
John, 46.
William, 28.
Walton, Bridget, 75.
John, 75.
Martha, 75.
Ward, Abigail, 25.
Parthania, 24.
Ware, Samuel, 42.
Warner, Priscilla, 6.
Samuel, 67, 68.
Warren, Daniel, 23, 46.
Hannah, 46.
Sarah, 23, 94.
Weare, Meshech, 12.
Webster, Samuel, 46.
Weld, Thomas, 82.
Wentworth, Benning, 8.
John, 11.
Moses, 33.
Weston, Ebenezer, 80.
Lucy, 80.
Wyman, 89.
Wheeler, Alice, 55.
Peter, 55.
Whipple, Susannah, 94.
Whitaker, Mary, 48, 77.
White, Hannah, 33.
Whiting, Dorothy, 91.
Elizabeth, 60.
Samuel, 60, 92.
Whitney, Aaron, 51.
Elizabeth, 23.
Hannah, 45.
James, 53, 63.
Jane, 47.
Joseph, 63.
Levi, 51.
Phineas, 71.
Rebecca, 63.
Sarah, 54.
Wiborne, Thomas, 36.
Wickham, Frederick, 77.
Wilkins, Andrew, 10.
Daniel, 10.
Hezekiah, 68.
Mehitable, 68.
Wilkinson, Ebenezer, 46.
Sarah, 46.
Willard, Samuel, 83.
Simon, 83.
Williams, Elizabeth, 68.
Isaac, 69.
Jason, 69.
John, 69.

Index.

Williams, Thomas, 68, 69.
Wilson, Elizabeth, 92.
  Jemima, 70.
  John, 92.
  Prudence, 89.
  Samuel, 69.
Winship, Josiah, 71.
  Noah, 71.
Winslow, Edward, 87.
  Hannah, 87.
  John, 87.
Withington, Samuel, 71.
Wood, Benjamin, 69.
Woodbridge, Martha, 93, 94.

Woodcock, William, 35.
Woods, Benjamin, 80.
  Daniel, 53.
  David, 70.
  Diademia, 72.
  John, 70.
  Mary, 72, 73.
  Nathaniel, 18.
  Oliver, 18, 53, 80.
  Samuel, 18.
  Sarah, 53, 78, 80.
  Solomon, 72, 73.
  Susannah, 73.
Woodward, Lydia, 46.
Woolderson, Frances, 25, 68.

Wright, Amaziah, 25.
  Ebenezer, 25.
  John, 29, 50.
  Joseph, 29.
  Mary, 32.
  Nehemiah, 50.
  Priscilla, 29.
Wyer, Daniel, 89.
Wyman, Abigail, 26.
  Hannah, 82.

Youngman, Nicholas, 32.
  Thomas, 32.

www.ingramcontent.com/pod-product-compliance
Lightning Source LLC
Chambersburg PA
CBHW060417090426
42734CB00011B/2343